THE GOLD
AND
THE GLORY

*The Story of Glenn Morris,
Olympic Champion and Movie Tarzan*

ALSO BY MIKE CHAPMAN

THE GOLD AND AND THE GLORY

The Story of Glenn Morris,
Olympic Champion and Movie Tarzan

By

Mike Chapman

CULTURE HOUSE BOOKS

THE GOLD AND THE GLORY

A Culture House Book / March, 2003

For information address: Culture House
                             P O Box 293
                             Newton, IA 50208

Library of Congress Cataloging-in-Publication Data
Chapman, Mike, 1943 -
    The Gold and The Glory / Mike Chapman
1. Morris, Glenn. 2. Tarzan. 3. WWII. 4. Colorado State University.
5. Movie History. 6. Simla, Colorado.

ISBN   0-9676080-4-X

PRINTED IN THE UNITED STATES OF AMERICA

First edition

*"Worldly fame is but a breath of wind
that blows now this way, and now that,
and changes names as it changes directions."*
— *Dante*

Acknowledgements

This book was nearly twenty years in the making, off and on, and involved lengthy correspondence and conversations with a number of people who cared a great deal about the life and times of Glenn Morris. At the head of that list is Morris D. Ververs, who has spent considerable energy in researching Glenn and keeping his memory alive. Ververs, a former Simla school principal, and his wife, Verna, a distant relative of Glenn's, graciously supplied a great deal of information and opened many doors for me in the community of Simla, Colorado. Others who assisted in the research of the book are Monty Gaddy, former editor of the Simla-based Ranchland News, and Ken Moore, athletic director at Simla Union High School. I also had the privilege of talking several times by phone to Glenn's brothers, Jack and Wayne, and his sister, Virginia Morris Baxter, as well as Caroline Edwards Tucker, the sister of Charlotte Edwards, Glenn's first wife. Frank Zarnowski, the nation's leading expert in the history of the decathlon, and Bob Mathias, legendary two-time Olympic champion, added valuable insights into Glenn's place in the history of the decathlon, the most demanding of all track events. Eleanor Holm graciously discussed via phone her memories of Glenn, both from the 1936 Olympics and while on the set of "Tarzan's Revenge."

One of the most powerful stories of the entire book was provided by Jim Larson, who was just a young sailor when he first met Glenn Morris during World War II; the story is incredible and I am deeply grateful to Jim for sharing it with the readers. In addition, Danton Burroughs, president of Edgar Rice Burroughs, Inc., in Tarzana, California, was extremely considerate in allowing me access to the huge collection of clippings and photos at ERB offices. Longtime ERB fan D. Peter Ogden was helpful in providing many of the great photos seen in the book. As always, George McWhorter, curator of the Burroughs collection at the University of Louisville, was a big help as I prepared the manuscript and sought photos. And I appreciate Denny Miller, one of the nicest men to ever play Tarzan, for reading a version of the story and offering some encouraging words.

On four occasions I visited the hometown of Glenn's youth, and I also traveled to Fort Collins on as many instances to walk over the area where he trained for the 1936 Olympic Games. I must give thanks to the small group of people in Simla who actually knew Glenn, and offered their recollections of him from nearly seven decades ago. They are rightfully proud of Glenn's accomplishments and accept him for who he was. The book would not have been near as complete or as interesting without the input of all these special folks.

Contents

Foreword

Growing up I had heard the names of most of the great American 1936 Berlin Olympians — names like Jesse Owens, Ken Carpenter, Earle Meadows, Cornelius Johnson, Forrest Towns and Glenn Morris.

It wasn't until May of 1948 that my coach, Virgil Jackson, convinced me that I should try the decathlon. The first meet was in early June, a week after I graduated from Tulare High School in Tulare, California. Somehow, I won that meet, and I thought that would be my one and only decathlon. But Coach Johnson stopped by my house a few days later and said that there was another decathlon meet the next month in Bloomfield, New Jersey. This was the national meet, and since 1948 was an Olympic year, it was also the Olympic trials. I finished first in that meet, and suddenly I was a member of the United States Olympic team. Because of World War II, no Olympic Games were held in 1940 and 1944…and London in 1948 still showed the ravishes of war. In early August, I won the London Olympic decathlon.

It was a fast and furious three months for me from the time my coach mentioned the decathlon until I won the Olympic gold medal. When I got back home, I realized that I didn't know a lot about the history of the Olympics, and especially any details about the decathlon itself, or the people who had competed in this event in Olympics past. I did know the name of Glenn Morris, and that he set the Olympic and World record in the 1936 Games, but I hadn't seen his actual marks for each of the ten events when he set the record.

After the London Games, I really thought that I would not compete in any more decathlons. Training was hard and time consuming and the 1952 Helsinki Games were four long years way. But when I finally saw Glenn's marks for the ten events, I changed my mind! His results so inspired me that from that moment Glenn became my idol and hero. I looked at his time in the 100 meters and thought that if I worked real hard for the next four years I could maybe run it as fast as he had. I did the same for the other nine events — and suddenly, for the first time in my life, I had a goal. That goal was to try to equal or better the marks of my newly-found idol. Somehow, two years later at a national decathlon meet in Tulare, I did break his world record. Then at the 1952 Helsinki Olympics, I broke his Olympic Games record, and also broke my own world record.

I would not have continued with the decathlon if it hadn't been for the inspiration that Glenn provided in his great performance in 1936. I always give credit to my coach, and to Glenn Morris, for helping me with a track and field event called the decathlon.

I had the chance to meet Glenn once at a sports banquet and had the privilege to talk to him for a while. As I recall, I said something like, "Gee, Glenn, I'm sorry I broke your record." He responded, "I'm glad you did, Bob. That's what records are made for, to be broken." Talking to him confirmed that he was a true gentleman and a great champion!

The Gold and The Glory tells about the life of this great champion. I enjoyed the book and there were many things that I didn't know about him. It's a fascinating story of growing up in Simla, Colorado, and his great sports career, culminating with his win at Berlin and his life after the Olympics.

Bob Mathias
Fresno, California
March 14, 2001

Preface

It's difficult to remember when I first became aware of Glenn Morris. I know that I saw his name in a magazine article in the 1950s with a list of Tarzan movie actors. I was very young and had just seen my first Tarzan film, staring Lex Barker, and it was not easy for me to envision anyone other than the handsome Barker as Tarzan; but the magazine article provided photos of ten actors who were, indeed, Tarzan. The list began with Elmo Lincoln in 1918, and continued with Gene Polar, P. Dempsey Tabler, James Pierce, Frank Merrill, Johnny Weissmuller, Buster Crabbe, Herman Brix, Glenn Morris and, finally, Lex Barker.

The article included a photo of Glenn Morris standing next to a majestic lion, and Glenn certainly looked the part of the legendary apeman. He was well muscled without being heavily muscled. He appeared lean and athletic, ready for action. Many years later, as sports editor of the Coloradoan newspaper in Fort Collins, Colorado, I came across his name again. While working one day at the sports desk, I received a phone call from a reader telling me that Glenn Morris had died in California. The caller thought I should mention that fact in the Fort Collins newspaper, since Glenn had been an athletic star at Colorado A&M College in the 1930s.

Colorado A&M, located in Fort Collins, had been renamed Colorado State University by the time I arrived. As sports editor of the local newspaper, I was closely involved with the school's athletic program. I traveled with the Colorado State University football and wrestling teams, was close friends with a number of coaches and athletes, and loved sports history. I wrote of Glenn's passing in a column and then, intrigued, began to do a bit of research.

As the years slipped by, I continued with my newspaper career, and also became involved with the Tarzan community. Even though my true sports passion is amateur wrestling (I am the founder of the International Wrestling Institute and Museum in Newton, Iowa, and have written twelve books on the sport), I have always been captivated by the decathlon event. I truly believe the Olympic decathlon champion is the greatest all-around athlete in the world. Ever since seeing the life stories of Jim Thorpe and Bob Mathias on the movie screen, I have marveled at the skills needed to be a decathlon champion….at any level. To just get through the grueling competition is a noteworthy achievement; to set a world record, as Glenn Morris did twice, and to win the gold medal in the Olympics, as he did in 1936, is to reach the pinnacle of athletic accomplishment. Many centuries ago, Homer said, "There is no greater glory for a man as long as he lives than that which he wins by his own hands and feet," and I subscribe to that statement wholeheartedly.

But I discovered that Glenn was more than just a superb athlete. He was involved in many activities at Simla High School, and was president of his senior class in college at Colorado A&M. He portrayed Tarzan in one film, and had a key role in another movie. He played briefly with the Detroit Lions of the NFL, and served as a naval officer in World War II, seeing extensive action in the South Pacific.

After the war, Glenn seemed to disappear from the national and world scene. No one knew much about the last twenty years of his life, and death came at an early age. Sporadically, I began to delve more into his background, and was fascinated with what I discovered. He was an enigmatic personality, admired by many, yet described as aloof and even arrogant by others. He seemed to be a multi-dimensional personality, trying to "find himself" in a complex world.

Glenn's story is full of gold and glory, and of descent and pathos. It began in tiny Simla, Colorado, and moved on to the world stage in Berlin. Included in the stirring saga are some of the world's most fascinating people — from the Olympic Games to Hollywood — and some of the most horrific events in world history.

Glenn Morris was like a comet shooting across the national horizon. He came from almost nowhere to achieve stunning fame, and then slipped back into obscurity. It is ironic that Germany was the setting of his greatest accomplishments and fame, and that an incredibly evil product of that country was also the root cause of his eventual demise, through the advent of World War II.

Along the research path, I received many encouraging words of support, from a variety of people who thought Glenn's story was worth telling in book form. One of the most important letters came from a career educator who has also spent many years following the Glenn Morris story: "We both like and appreciate the fact that you have contributed significantly to the historical knowledge of an extraordinary individual and the events surrounding him," wrote Morris D. Ververs, referring to his wife, Verna, as well. "A fascinating story would have been lost forever had you not proceeded with writing this book."

It is my hope that Glenn Morris will be viewed as a man who desperately wanted to rise above his humble beginnings and worked indefatigably to realize his dreams, but was ultimately overwhelmed by events beyond his control. It is not a tragic story, it is simply a story about life as seen through the fortunes, good and bad, of an intriguing figure. I hope you enjoy getting to know Glenn Morris as much as I did.

Mike Chapman,
October 20, 2002

The Zenith

The sun over Germany broke through the clouds briefly and cast its glow on Leni Riefenstahl as she walked across the grassy carpet of the marvelous new sports stadium. There was a slight breeze stirring, and the Berlin crowd was beginning to fill the stands. Soon, there would be nearly one hundred thousand sports enthusiasts in the huge stadium, one of the most impressive athletic arenas ever constructed in the history of mankind.

It was August 7, 1936, and Leni was in her glory. Certainly, no one could blame her for feeling flush with excitement and pride. After all, the famed actress/photographer/filmmaker had been given unlimited access to hundreds of athletes at the greatest sporting event of all time. With the explicit approval of Chancellor Adolph Hitler, the German government had gone all out to create an Olympic Games showcase that would hopefully never be surpassed, and certainly never forgotten. It was Leni's privilege and duty to record the events on film, to be seen around the world for decades and decades to come!

A vivacious beauty who had appeared in many German films but now preferred life behind the camera, Leni was busily setting up her equipment and planning her day's schedule when she glanced across the stadium. She instantly ceased what she was doing, and stared at an athlete striding across the grassy field some fifty yards from her. The lean and muscular American was the most magnificent physical specimen she had ever laid eyes on. He was on his way to the warm-up area, staring straight ahead, focused on the mission he had come nearly six thousand miles to complete.

Glenn Morris had journeyed to mighty Berlin from the dusty streets of a tiny town on the plains of Colorado to strive for Olympic gold and Olympic glory in the grueling decathlon, and he was determined to let nothing distract him. Then he glanced sideways, and caught sight of the beautiful woman across the field. From that moment on, he seemed to have two overwhelming goals — first, to become an Olympic champion and, secondly, to meet Leni Riefenstahl.

In a matter of days, all of his dreams and hopes would come to fruition. Glenn Morris of Simla, Colorado, would dazzle the huge crowds in Berlin, and even Hitler himself….as well as Hitler's precocious mistress, Eva Braun. Morris would taste the nectar of the Olympians in a fashion few others would ever know. He would ascend to the mountaintop in meteoric fashion…and then cling precariously to the pinnacle before beginning an equally rapid and stunning descent.

But first, there was Berlin, Hitler, the decathlon…..and Leni.

Many historians consider the Berlin Olympics the most intriguing of all athletic competitions, and it would be easy to concur with that point of view. These Games had it all — a ruthless dictator destined to become the most despised man of the 20th century, the feared Nazi symbols, the mysterious Eva Braun, the majesty of an imperial nation about to explode onto the world scene, the mighty Hindenberg dirigible hovering overhead, and incredible pageantry. The Games also had Jesse Owens, one of the most celebrated athletes ever to grace an Olympic stadium…and the Games also had Glenn Morris, one of the most magnificent champions in Olympic history.

Leni spent the following two weeks filming the greatest stars of the eleventh Olympiad, and chronicling the exploits of these legendary athletes. The subject that intrigued her the very most was the incredibly driven young man from Simla, Colorado.

"Morris competed like a man possessed," wrote Frank Zarnowski in his book, *The Decathlon*. "His aggressiveness and grim determination, matched in later Olympics only by Bruce Jenner, was captured by Leni Riefenstahl's film, 'Olympiad, Festival of Nations.'"

Riefenstahl's film offers a compelling study of Morris at his athletic best — swift, lean and focused like few athletes of any era. He is shown running, leaping, throwing and vaulting. Appearing almost gaunt at times, it's surprising to note he had weighed nearly one hundred and ninety pounds before leaving the United States for the Atlantic crossing on the ship USS Manhattan, along with sixty-six other United States track and field athletes comprising the 1936 Olympic squad.

Morris had seen his first decathlon in 1935 and was captivated by the spectacle. A grueling two-day showcase of pure athletic skill and stamina, the event includes ten individual athletic contests designed to test an athlete's overall ability and resolve, to the highest degree. The Berlin decathlon began August 7 with the 100-yard dash and added the long jump, shot put, high jump and 4,300 meters, all on the first day. The second day dawned cold and wet, offering miserable conditions for any track and field athlete. It began with the 110 high hurdles, and followed with the discus throw, pole vault, javelin, and concluded with the exhausting 1,500-meter run.

Competing in only his third decathlon, Morris took control on the second day and stormed to a world record of 7,900 points. He defeated the runner-up, Robert Clark, also of the United States, by a margin of 299 points! Miss Braun herself placed the laurel wreath on his head, and reportedly was enamored of him, in much the same fashion as was Leni Riefenstahl. Morris had won his Olympic gold medal in a fashion that few who were there would ever forget, bringing nearly one hundred thousand fans roaring to their feet, and exciting at least two very notable German women in the process.

By the time the Olympic fever began to wane, Morris had conquered nearly everything in sight. He was star of a ticker tape parade in New York City and Denver, and the state of Colorado declared Glenn Morris Day. He was the winner of the prestigious Sullivan Award, presented by the Amateur Athletic Union (AAU) to the top amateur athlete in the country. National newspapers and movie-house newsreels boasted of his accomplishments. He was front-page news in both of the large Denver newspapers of the day. On September 9, 1936, the Simla Sun devoted its entire front page to its favorite son, and signs proclaiming his fame were placed on Highway 24 leading into Simla. Promoters and Barnums of all persuasion courted him. Hollywood came calling, and so did the National Football League.

In the autumn and winter of 1936, the gold and the glory were overflowing for Glenn Morris. And it all began on a small bean farm near Simla, Colorado.

Simla and Fort Collins

Simla, Colorado, hardly seems the place where Olympic dreams are born and nurtured. The origins of the tiny little town, situated in the eastern lowlands some fifty miles east of Colorado Springs, are less than storybook sweet. The original inhabitants of the region were rugged, nomadic Indian tribes — Kiowa, Ute, Cheyenne, Arapaho, Blackfoot and Jicarilla Apache. They eased their way along the South Platte and Arkansas rivers, eking out a bare existence by hunting and foraging. Explorers Zebulon Pike and Stephen H. Long passed through the area on their way to discovering peaks which were subsequently named for them. But they saw nothing which interested them in staying beyond a night.

Long called the Simla plains area of eastern Colorado "The Great American Desert." The declaration went a long way toward discouraging any would-be settlers from locating in the area for decades to come. But the discovery of gold in 1858 opened up the entire state and an estimated 100,000 miners poured into Colorado. The native Indians, upset and frightened by the great influx, rebelled, and a number of deadly skirmishes resulted. By the late 1870s, eastern Colorado was largely settled, however, and ranchers and dryland farmers followed in the miners' wake.

Simla was born out of the railroad invasion that came on the heels of the settlers. Originally, it was little more than a site for dumping unused railroad cars on the Rock Island line. The town received its name in a rather curious fashion: the twelve-year-old daughter of a Rock Island executive called it Simla after reading the name in a book about India as she traveled through the area. The nearby town of Ramah was named in similar fashion.

The year 1912 marked several milestones in the somewhat sparse historical saga of Simla. It's the year the little village became incorporated, when Lee L. Stewart became its first mayor, and when the Simla Union High School district was formed. In addition, the area high school was moved from nearby Matheson to Simla, and the first church was built.

It was also the year its most famous citizen, Glenn Edgar Morris, was born several hundred miles to the east. He entered the world on June 18, in St. Louis, Missouri, the second of seven children born to John and Emma Morris. John and Emma lived several years in their native Missouri but, when Glenn was three, the family moved to Colorado in search of a better life. What they found in Simla was a hard existence, about as hard as one can imagine at that time in America.

The very summer Glenn Morris first saw the light of day, an Indian who had been raised in a Sac and Fox tribe in Oklahoma was making a name for himself that would endure for all time in the world of sport. When Jim Thorpe won his Olympic decathlon gold medal in Stockholm, Sweden, on July 10, 1912 — and nodded politely as King Gustav called him the greatest athlete in the world — Morris was less than a month old. But twenty-four years later, Morris would run in the footsteps of the great Thorpe, and draw similar raves from the Chancellor of Germany, a man the world would come to despise as much as it idolized Thorpe.

"Little did John Francis Morris and Emma Rodett Lacy realize when they married that their union would bring forth a unique set of inherited traits in a son," wrote Morris family historian Jean Bird, Glenn's cousin, in 1980. "These traits, and the contributions of their own dedicated family life and principles, and the initiative and desire to work and succeed by their son, would culminate in one boy destined to be named as the world's 'most perfect athlete.'" *(1)*

Life in Simla was rough in the years Glenn Morris was growing up. The 160-acre farm where his parents were engaged in raising pinto beans was located some three miles north of town, along a dirt road that was often difficult to traverse, and nearly impossible after spring storms. Like most farm families in the area, the Morris clan was always struggling to make enough money to scratch out even a meager existence. Jack and Glenn often went to school in clothes that had been mended by Emma, and spending-money was almost non-existent. There was always plenty of work to do on the farm, but Glenn preferred to read and daydream about athletic exploits.

Bird wrote that "by the time Glenn was twelve, he could handle three milk cows a day. His real interest, though, was in physical excellence. He searched for books and characters with athletics as their subject of interest." *(2)*

"We were a sort of poor family out there in eastern Colorado," recalled his older brother Jack in 1989. "We were all a very close-knit family, except Glenn. He was always different, something special, really. He was always looking ahead to better things. He and Dad sometimes had some real set-tos; Glenn never wanted to go out and hoe beans, or that sort of thing.

"Dad was president of the school board for awhile, and the Morris family was pretty well-known in the parts. We rated around that area. I was the one who made the straight As in school. Glenn got to make the Cs because he was working so hard on athletics."

Jack recalled the long treks to and from school as playing a key role in his brother's athletic development.

"We walked to school, hiked it in summer and winter. Glenn may have run some days to school, but I doubt he ran back. It was uphill and would have been real tough coming back. But he was always doing something around the farmyard. He had a high jump pit and a long jump pit he made, and he also made some hurdles out of sticks, and what have you. And he had a chinning bar in the yard he was always working on."

His mother made his first high school track uniform for him. Glenn had wanted to buy a class ring for two dollars and fifty cents, but didn't have the money. The bleak poverty was undoubtedly a major force in determining his outlook on life, and left an indelible stamp on him. It inspired him to set goals and dream of moving beyond Simla, and to improve his lot in life.

But there were obstacles to overcome besides the abject poverty. Glenn was afflicted with asthma. At times it would become so severe that he would collapse on the ground, clutching his chest and fighting for breath. It was a sight that terrified his mother, but it seems to have done even more to fuel the fire inside Glenn. More than anything, he wanted to defeat the problems that seemed to engulf him. Asthma and poverty were mere challenges to be overcome, and he had the formula: It was work, and work, and work — harder than anyone else around him. As the years slipped by, the resolve was forged into a steely determination that bordered on obsession.

"He had goals," said Jack quietly. "He wanted to set the state record in the hurdles. He was already the best by far in Simla and around that area, but he wanted to be best in the state. He worked feverishly on that goal.

"In football, I was a miserable guard," recalled Jack. "It was my job to go out there and throw the blocks for the guys with the ball. Glenn was a back, racing downfield and catching the passes."

Like the young Jim Thorpe of Oklahoma two decades earlier, Glenn could often be seen running down the lonely stretch of road near the farm, hurdling over sagging fences, and leaping a narrow creek that ran near the Morris property. Running became a way of life....a means of finding solace in the driving of one's body against the wonders of nature — to run like a wild stag, free and powerful.

"There weren't any school buses in those days," said Virgil Richardson, an uncle who lived all his life in Simla, to a newspaper reporter in 1984. "A lot of kids from a long ways off used to stay with families in town. But not Glenn. For him, it was no problem. He just ran."

He raced against Jack, when chores were completed, or any neighbors who happened by. Bill Moreland, an older cousin who worked a farm close to the Morris home, recognized the latent talent in the youngster and offered encouragement. Moreland constructed two makeshift hurdles for Morris to leap over. A former shot putter and discus thrower, Moreland also provided his young and eager protege with his first rudimentary instructions in those events.

Later on, he also benefited from working with a coach/teacher named Burton Clammer, who had starred in track at the University of Colorado in Boulder. Like Moreland before him, Clammer took a personal interest in Morris, perhaps sensing the vast potential that lay hidden in the lean body. He took Glenn under his wing and encouraged him to set high goals and to work even harder. Coaches would always play an important role in his early successes.

At Simla High School, Morris did well in nearly all he attempted, on the athletic field and off. He was a member of the student council and of the annual staff all four years of high school, acted in the school play as a junior, and was a member of Hi-Y. His senior year, 1930, he was editor-in-chief of the school newspaper. He lettered three years each in track and basketball, and twice in football, where he played right halfback on a team that suffered from a lack of players and finished less than .500 both years.

"One thing that hindered progress was the fact that scarcely ever two full teams were out for practice," reported the 1930 high school yearbook.

Morris played the "tip-off position" in basketball. Competing in small, bleak gyms against the other tiny schools sprinkled across the plains of eastern Colorado, the Simla squad won more than half its games.

"He wasn't a real good shooter, but he played a good floor game," recalled J.J. (Swede) Moreland, Bill's younger brother. "Track was his best sport. We lived on the next farm over, and if you went over to play with him and the other Morris kids, Glenn was doing something all the time. He was always wanting to race or jump, or do something like that."

In the 1930 Eastern Colorado League (ECL) high school track meet held in Burlington, Glenn gave an indication of what could be in his future. He won first place in six different events and set records in the high jump and the discus. He scored 33 points in the meet all by himself.

He concluded his Simla athletic career by placing third in the state meet in the low hurdles. For years he had dreamed of being the state champion; he had not achieved his goal, but he had come close. More importantly, he realized he could compete at a high level and that the key to success in athletics was his willingness to work hard and long.

Though he was certainly above average in football and basketball, there was nothing about Morris that suggested he had the potential to become the greatest athlete in the world just six years later. But the young Simla athlete's potential lay in his versatility, which was obvious to all who saw him compete, and in his focus, which was obvious only to those who knew him well. By all accounts, Morris was quiet and introspective, driven by an inner hunger. Like all great athletes before and since, he had the ability to push himself harder than those around him in his quest for excellence.

As the years slipped by, that inner hunger would prove to be a double-edged sword. It would help him become a superb athlete…..but it would also prove to be a characteristic that would be extremely difficult to deal with as the athletic opportunities and goals dimmed. His intense drive was channeled into athletics for the first half of his life; later, problems developed as the intense drive — an obsession, really — began its search for an outlet other than athletics. Even in his youth, he was described as "different" by those who knew him well, and "moody" by at least one family member.

Both Cledys Moore, who played on the same Simla football team with Glenn and was a year behind him in school, and Swede Moreland felt there was something "different" about him as he was growing up in Simla.

"He wasn't very talkative," said Moore in 2000. "He wasn't bashful, but he sure wasn't outgoing, like Jack was. Glenn was more of an observer. He liked to watch other people, quietly, and think about things. He was…..just different, I guess."

Jean Bird recalled that during his early years, Glenn didn't always appreciate his Morris relatives when they converged upon the family farm. "He was shy and didn't encourage their attentions," she wrote. *(3)* Brother Jack also hinted that Glenn often kept himself at a distance from the family.

Of course, there were some advantages (and also disadvantages) to being the town's star athlete. Glenn found himself growing popular with the young girls around

Simla…..and also having to defend his reputation at times against the town toughs.

"You got along better with the gals if you were an athlete in those days," Jack said, with a chuckle. "And Glenn was always good with the girls."

Glenn apparently had a pugilistic side to his nature, as well as a romantic side. Bird reported that the two Morris boys were forced to take up boxing to learn how to defend themselves.

"Glenn planned to buy a pair of boxing gloves," Bird wrote. "He and Jack had been jumped by some boys in town and they hadn't fared too well. Glenn began working out on neighbor's farms during the summer. He purchased the boxing gloves and a Charles Atlas training kit to boot. He believed the Charles Atlas training would help him develop finger and hand strength. He vowed the boys in town had better look out from then on." *(4)*

Jack doesn't remember the purchase of boxing gloves by Glenn, but does recollect minor scuffles from time to time while growing up in Simla.

"We had some tussles in eighth or ninth grade that I recall, with some wiseacres," said Jack. "I was always smaller than Glenn, and he took the front in those types of things. But we didn't have much trouble of that kind."

When Glenn graduated from high school on May 16, 1930, the nation was in the iron grip of the Great Depression, and Colorado was in the middle of the Dust Bowl. The two forces combined to make life exceedingly difficult for dryland farmers in the western plains, and the Morris family certainly was no exception.

But Jack and Glenn Morris were in a unique situation due to their athletic talents. While college was a far-off dream for many in the Simla area, Jack used his football skills as a way to get into Colorado State Teachers College (now the University of Northern Colorado) in Greeley. And Glenn's natural athletic ability and his desire to get ahead provided the opportunity for him to acquire a college education. Athletic scholarships had not yet been implemented, but college coaches wrote letters to athletes who interested them. The coaches invited them to their college and offered to help them in any way they could, such as finding jobs that paid a decent wage.

Glenn settled on Colorado State College in Fort Collins, about eighty miles northwest of Simla. The school opened its doors in 1879 as State Agriculture College, with five students. In 1935, it became known as Colorado State College of Agriculture and Mechanical Arts (A&M). The final name change came in 1957, to Colorado State University. By the year 2000, the college nestled in the foothills could boast of nearly 25,000 students.

Morris arrived on campus in the fall of 1930, a lean six foot, two inches tall. But his 182-pound frame was draped with raw muscle; fed with hard work and determination, it would mature over the next six years into a splendid athletic machine. He was that rare collegiate athlete able to compete at a varsity level in three different sports, going from one season to the next with scarcely a break. He competed in football, basketball and track as a freshman, but dropped basketball after just one season to concentrate on the other two sports.

At Colorado State College, as in Simla, Morris worked hard on developing his athletic skills. Quiet and somewhat aloof, he quickly developed a strong mentor-pupil relationship with football coach Harry Hughes, who doubled as track coach in the spring and was also athletic director. Together, without realizing it, they laid the foundation for Olympic stardom, beginning with their first meeting when Morris was a freshman at the opening day of football practice.

"He was as green as the stadium grass, but I knew in a glance I had a natural born athlete in the rough," Hughes recalled years later. "Yes siree, that boy carried plenty of dynamite. He was as quick on his feet as a cat, and he had a hair-trigger mind."

Morris made the freshman team at right end and was moved up to the varsity early in the season. He held the position for the next three years of varsity action, and also played defensive back. In his first varsity conference game at home as a sophomore, he caught ten passes from quarterback Albert (Red) White. His junior year, he caught the second longest touchdown pass in the nation.

"He was a terrific end," said brother Jack. "Since I went to Greeley (about forty-five miles southeast of Fort Collins), I didn't get to see him play much. The one time I remember best is the year his team came down to play us. He caught a tremendous pass for a touchdown, about 80 yards....and that's what beat us. I had mixed emotions, of course, but I was pretty proud of him.

"After the game, I asked him, 'How on earth did you catch that pass? It was way over your head.' And he said, 'There's a rule that you should catch anything you can touch. I had to catch that ball!'"

Like all athletes in the 1930s, Glenn worked his way through college. He found a job at the school's printing shop and started out by delivering printed items on a bike. Before long, however, he was moved inside the plant and began working on a machine. He joined the Alpha Tau Omega fraternity and was involved in many aspects of campus life. His quiet manner and good looks made him popular; he was elected secretary of his sophomore class. His senior year, he was voted president of the Associated Students, which was the student council. The 1936 college yearbook, *Silver Spruce*, offers a dozen photos of him, including a full-page facial photograph in a special section labeled "*Pacemakers*."

Following his final season of football, Morris earned All-Rocky Mountain honors and was selected to play in the prestigious 1934 East-West Shrine game in San Francisco. Years later, Hughes said Morris was the best end he ever coached and picked him for his all-time Colorado State College team.

The young man from Simla undoubtedly could have begun a career in professional football....had it not been for his blossoming track skills, and expectations. In his final track season, he broke conference records in the low and high hurdles. At the Colorado intercollegiate meet in Boulder, he turned in an amazing performance. He placed in eleven events for the Aggies.

Shortly after, he experienced an event that fired his imagination and changed the direction of his life. Competing in the Kansas Relays of 1935 as a hurdler, he saw the decathlon for the first time. The demanding beauty of the ten events captivated him, and brought back memories of his youth, racing down the lane at the family farm, dreaming of athletic glory.

He had read of Jim Thorpe's remarkable exploits in 1912, and he had heard ath-

LEFT: The old Simla High School, where Glenn Morris attended classes, graduating in 1930.

Glenn is seen in his senior class photo (above), as a junior football player (right) and in the football team photo (below) his senior year, 1929. He is in the first row, holding the ball.

(Photos courtesy of Monty Gaddy and Simla Union High School)

Glenn Morris

LEFT: Glenn was a member of the school newspaper staff, wearing his Simla lettersweater for the photo.

RIGHT: He was active in many school activities, as shown in this photo from the Simla yearbook.

BOTTOM: Glenn was a member of the basketball squad for three seasons (front row, third from right).

GLENN MORRIS

Track 2-3-4
Hi-Y
Basketball 2-3-4
Football 3-4
S Club 2-3-4
Student Council 4
Junior Play
Annual Staff 4

ABOVE: Morris was an all-conference end in college and played in the East-West All-Star game his senior year.

RIGHT: Harry Hughes was football coach during Glenn's years at Colorado State A&M. He was also best man in Glenn's wedding.

These pictures were taken from the 1936 *Silver Spruce,* the yearbook for Colorado State College. Charlotte Edwards (above) was a junior at the time, while Glenn Morris was one of the seven seniors singled out for a full page in the section called *Pacemakers* (right). He was also president of The Associated Students (bottom).

THE ASSOCIATED STUDENTS

GLENN MORRIS
President
Associated Students

President	GLENN MORRIS
Vice-President	SIDNEY COWAN
Second Vice-President	JULIA REED
Secretary	CHESTER LAIRD

A constitution and by-laws were drawn up by the Associated Students of the Colorado Agricultural College in 1917. This association was organized to promote and regulate the student activities on the campus.

The Student Council acts as the executive body of the students and recommends to the student body important measures to be taken. The Council is composed of five seniors, four juniors, three sophomores and two freshmen.

**Glenn was a one-man track team at
Colorado State College, participating in the
discus (top photo), sprints (left)
and shot put (above).**

(Colorado State University Archives)

Glenn Morris

Shortly after this photo was taken on the Colorado State A&M campus in the summer of 1936, Glenn Morris would be recognized as the greatest all-around athlete in the world.

(Colorado State University Archives)

Prior to leaving for Berlin, Glenn sits on the back steps of the fieldhouse at South College Avenue on the Colorado State College campus in Fort Collins, where he had done all his training for the Olympic Games.
(Colorado State University Archives)

letes talk with great respect about the decathlon. Years later, there were stories that Glenn had actually attended the 1932 Olympic Games in Los Angeles, and watched from the stands as Jim Bausch set a world record and captured the gold medal. "I can do better than that," he reportedly told friends (Simla Sun, Sept. 9, 1936, page 1).

But Jack doubts Glenn actually went all the way to Los Angeles: "I don't think he had the money or the time for such a trip," said his brother in 1989. Whether or not he actually went to the Olympics in 1932, Glenn was driven by the power and beauty of the decathlon by 1935. Upon leaving the Kansas Relays that year, he was determined to test himself soon in the grueling event.

"He told Hughes he thought he could do those events better than the fellow who had won (at Kansas)," wrote Mike Monroe of the Denver Post in 1984. "Hughes told Morris he'd help. Morris had never tried the pole vault and the mile run. But a year later, he returned to the Kansas Relays...."

First, though, he won the prestigious Nye Award as the top athlete on campus, and then graduated with a degree in economics and sociology. He took a job as a car salesman in Fort Collins to support himself. He also became a graduate assistant coach in both football and basketball, and began studying the decathlon. He rented a room in a boarding house just two blocks north of the track and fieldhouse, on the same side of the street. The room at 637 South College Avenue, in the very heart of Fort Collins, gave him easy access to the training facility, and he took great advantage of its proximity. He trained with zeal — running, vaulting and leaping at the track on South College Avenue. In poor weather, he would move inside the large building, and work for hours on the various events. Glenn Morris had become obsessed with proving himself in the most demanding athletic event devised by man.

Two men who could not forget the impression Glenn Morris left on them were Norman Cable and John Morrell. Cable had entered Colorado State College in 1934 as a freshman, and Morrell was a young boy when he first encountered Morris.

"When I was a freshman and varsity football player, Glenn took a great interest in my development as team punter," recalled Cable in 2001. "Like Glenn, I also played what we called strong-side end. We competed against each other in practice sessions, sending our booming punts high and long down the field." Cable watched with deep respect as Morris trained for the decathlon, and was full of pride when his friend and mentor made the team and sailed for Berlin.

Morrell lived in Fort Collins for most of his life. After becoming a medical doctor, he served as team physician for Colorado State University football teams in the 1970s.

"I would see him in the South College fieldhouse, late at night, working out," said Morrell, his voice edged with admiration even after nearly six decades. "He was so impressive. I remember once, he had on regular school clothes. He was looking at the high jump bar, then moved back a few steps, eyed it, and then ran up and leaped over it, in school clothes.

"Glenn Morris was a great athlete," said Morrell, with awe in his voice. "He was also a dapper dresser and a handsome man. He was really something; yes, he was."

Bob Pike was another familiar sight around Fort Collins athletics for decades, both on the high school and college levels. As a physician, he devoted thousands of hours to sports programs of all types. Like Morrell, Pike also harbored fond memories of Morris.

"He was a superb athlete, maybe the best this state ever produced," said Pike. "He starred in football and track, and was a good basketball player, too. And then to win the Olympic gold medal in the decathlon....what an accomplishment. Like John Morrell, I remember watching him as a youngster and being very, very impressed by him. He was just something special."

After graduation, Morris's lean, hard body began to pack on additional muscle, and adapted itself to the challenge ahead. But he also put his sharp analytical mind to work, as well.

"A keen student of form, Glenn quickly realized the need for relaxation in conserving his strength during the grueling decathlon," wrote Leonard Cahn for the Denver Post in 1936. "He found the answer one day in the spring of 1935 while giving pointers to a group of Aggie athletes. His pupils were running hard while Morris, exerting no unnatural effort, was striding along by their side.

"'Why, I can run faster this way than I could when I was bearing down. That's the secret,' he told himself."

Basically a hurdler and sprinter since his days back in Simla, Morris traveled to the 1935 Junior Nationals and the 1935 Senior Nationals to compete in the 400-meter hurdles. He won first in the Juniors and placed third in the Seniors. He also took good advantage of the opportunity to study the other track athletes in the other disciplines of the decathlon. He realized that while he was a good hurdler, he was not fast enough to become world-class. But, he felt hard work was the real key to success in the decathlon...and he was convinced he could outwork any other athlete.

With the next Olympics only a year away, he set his sights on the gold medal. And once he dedicated himself to the decathlon, there was no holding back. He centered his entire life around the pursuit of excellence – running constantly, setting up the hurdles, throwing the shot and discus, and working on the gymnastics rings to improve his pole vaulting skills. He read all he could about track techniques and even wrote to coaches he admired, asking questions. He mapped out a schedule and stuck to it like clockwork. He kept a golf ball in his pocket, squeezing it constantly to develop finger strength. He began walking on his hands to improve his arm strength and his sense of balance, both essential ingredients in the pole vault, the event likely to pose his biggest challenge.

"He lived and slept decathlon," wrote Cahn. "The pole vault was his hardest event and even now he hasn't mastered the art of falling correctly. Many nights he limped under the showers after taking bad spills, but he came out the next afternoon determined to improve."

He was also deriving strength and support from a brand new source. At a campus dance his senior year, he had met a young Colorado State College co-ed named Charlotte Edwards. An attractive, petite brunette from Sterling, Colorado, she was a class behind him. She was majoring in home economics and planning on becoming a schoolteacher. They began dating and in a short amount of time were going steady. He shared his Olympic dream with her and she was very supportive. In fact, she become involved on a very personal level. She mapped out a diet to aid him with providing sufficient nutrition, and even accompanied him on his grueling workouts.

"Charlotte had several other guys who were crazy about her, but she was fascinated with Glenn Morris," said Charlotte's sister, Caroline Tucker, from her home in Valencia, California in January of 2001. "She really helped him. She would go to the track with him and time him, and then go home and prepare special meals. She was really involved."

"Sometimes, I was able to cook for him and other times the landlady at his boarding house prepared the menus I prescribed," Charlotte told a newspaper reporter in 1936. "I made him quit all starches except whole wheat bread and eat meat twice a day with stewed fruits. He lost ten pounds but said he was stronger than ever.

"We worked out two hours every day, no matter what the weather. I would start him on his distance runs, then dash across the field and shout at him after he rounded the turn, the time he was making. Then I would run across the field to see how he finished.

"I lost ten pounds myself," she said.

Charlotte's faith in him and commitment to the goal meant a great deal to Glenn as he worked indefatigably to be the best he could be. He told a reporter that while others had scoffed at his Olympic dreams, she had been by his side all during his training. It was obviously a shared dream and team effort that brought the two young students close together, both on and off the field.

When he returned to the Kansas Relays on April 15 of 1936 for his first crack at the decathlon, he was a pure athletic talent waiting to explode. At Lawrence, he ran over the field and established an American decathlon record with a total of 7,576 points. He stunned the onlookers with his first day's performance, but suffered a pulled muscle in his right leg in the fifth event.

"That night, they worked on his leg until 10 o'clock and he slept but little," wrote Cahn. "The next day he went right out and won the hurdles and the discus and there was no stopping him after that. In less than forty-eight hours, he had leaped from obscurity to prominence in the banner headlines of every sports page in the land, champion of champions in the toughest, most grueling test developed by man."

Among the great athletes he outscored in Kansas was a former University of Chicago football star named Jay Berwanger. Just the year previous, Berwanger had become the first-ever recipient of a new football award called the Heisman Trophy. In fact, Berwanger was the model for the famous sculpture, which portrays a powerful running back throwing a stiff arm at an imaginary foe.

"I remember Glenn Morris well," said Berwanger in 1988, sitting in his office in Downer's Grove, Illinois, some fifty-two years later. "He was a great all-around athlete. That day, he was head and shoulders above the field, including me!"

Back in Fort Collins, Glenn was busy preparing for what would be the single greatest event of his life, in terms of fulfillment and satisfaction. The victory in Kansas had qualified him for the Olympic trials in Milwaukee, Wisconsin. He was riding a personal high, feeling good about himself, his romance with Charlotte, and with his athletic prospects. Though the Olympic fever was nothing like it would become in later years, with the advent of television, it was still a very popular diversion in the spring of 1936.

Flush with victory at Kansas, Morris was filled with confidence and was anticipating a wonderful athletic and educational experience in the Olympics. He had even gone so far as to begin reading travel books on Germany.

"I'm going to know something about the old world before I take the boat," he told the Denver Post. "This trip means more to me than just an athletic jaunt."

But before getting to Germany, he had to pass through Milwaukee. The Olympic decathlon trials were set for June 5-6. Competing in Marquette Stadium, Morris fell behind Robert Clark of the San Francisco Olympic Club in the early going. But he set a personal record of six foot one and one-half inches in the high jump, the fourth event, to pull into a tie with the Californian. Then, in the final event of the first day, he passed Clark with a tremendous 50.7-second effort in the 400 meters.

To start the second day, he nearly fouled out of the competition with two misses in the pole vault, his worst event. But he showed his mettle and hit eleven feet, four inches in his final attempt. With a nervous Harry Hughes coaching at his side the entire time, Morris finished the day with 7,880 points — good for first place and a new world record!

With the performance, Morris became the first Olympian in any sport from the state of Colorado. He also established himself as one of the two favorites for the Olympic gold medal. His main competition was expected to be German star Hans Sievert, holder of the world record up until the moment Morris hit the tape in the final event in Milwaukee.

Two days after setting the world record, Morris was back in Fort Collins, but hardly resting. He walked nearly twenty miles on a fishing expedition with friends, and remarked the trip was even more exhausting than competing in the decathlon. He may have been fishing, but his mind certainly was on the incredible adventure that lay ahead. And so were the thoughts of many Colorado fans across the state. Hundreds banded together to raise money to help pay his expenses to Berlin.

On July 4, the young man from Simla said goodbye to Charlotte and a small circle of friends, and left Fort Collins for New York City. He met the head coach, Lawson Robertson of Pittsburgh, and other members of the team. He also met Jesse Owens, who was about to become one of the most revered athletes in Olympic history, and the huge discus thrower, Ken Carpenter, who would become his closest confidant on the trip. He also was introduced to a petite swimmer named Eleanor Holm, unaware of how their paths would converge two years later in Hollywood.

As he boarded the USS Manhattan for the nine-day ocean voyage, Glenn's mind was filled with thoughts of gold and glory in faraway Germany. He could have had no idea of how the trip might change his entire life, in ways he could never imagine.

The Berlin Olympics

The world may never again see a spectacle quite like the Summer Olympics of 1936. The combination of world events had been set in motion which would bring about the single most calamitous event in the history of the world. And yet, for the fourteen days (August 2-16) of the Summer Games, the citizens of the world seemed to pause, collectively catching their breath.

The Berlin Olympics was a magnificent project, from start to finish. Adolph Hitler spared no expense in his determination to impress the world with Nazi style and power. Some thirty-five years later, IOC President Avery Brundage still considered the Berlin Olympics the "finest in modern history."

In the final report of the Games, the United States official position was just as glowing as was Brundage's:

"The Games of the XIth Olympiad at Berlin, Germany, was the greatest and most glorious athletic festival ever conducted, the most spectacular and colossal of all time. The estimated attendance for the entire period of the Games was 3,500,000. Great credit is due to Germany's brilliant feat of organization." *(5)*

The Games were also shrouded in tense and stirring controversy. Anti-Semitism was made national policy by Hitler in 1935, stripping all Jews in Germany of civil rights and their citizenship. Many U.S. groups urged a boycott of the Games, and the United States Congress considered a resolution which pushed for a boycott, but voted it down. The powerful Amateur Athletic Union, the nation's leading amateur sports organization, offered a petition with 500,000 names requesting that the United States skip the Games.

The conflict even raged in the host country of Germany.

"Some were opposed on the grounds that visitors would see and be repelled by the authoritarian rule, and Germany would thereby lose friends," wrote the authors of *Pursuit of Excellence: The Olympic Story*. "Heinrich Himmler, head of the SS security force, urged against having the Games, but propaganda chief Joseph Goebbels countered him, arguing that it was a chance to impress a watching world favorably." *(6)*

The German hierarchy argued among itself for a number of months. Finally, Hitler made the decision that the Olympics would indeed come to Nazi Germany. He also declared that no expense would be spared in the quest to show to the world the might of his beloved Aryan race.

"Whatever may have been the general atmosphere surrounding the Games, no one could deny the vast, almost overwhelming enthusiasm of the crowds. Nothing to equal the popular interest had ever been seen in Olympic history," wrote Bill Henry in his book, *An Approved History of the Olympic Games.* (7)

With an estimated four million citizens, Berlin was the fourth largest city in the world, and the Nazi-controlled government went all out to impress its visitors. The city was cleaned and spruced up at the cost of millions of dollars, and citizens were told by the Nazi officials to go out of their way to be courteous and friendly to their visitors. More than 300,000 foreign visitors flooded the area, along with 5,300 athletes representing fifty-one nations.

The United States Olympic Committee was a group of crusty men, many in their fifties. Led by Brundage – a former Olympian himself (he had participated in the pentathlon in 1912, competing against the likes of Jim Thorpe and George Patton) – the group members saw themselves as the lords of the Games. They enjoyed tremendous authority, and more than just a bit of arrogance has been attributed to their actions.

These men viewed Morris as the perfect example of the Olympian spirit. He was everything they could have hoped for – photogenic, articulate but not too talky (and likely to get in trouble with the press), and dedicated to the task at hand. The Colorado comet had only one goal in mind, and that was to stamp himself as the greatest athlete in the world. He was reserved and polite, their ideal of the young American athlete on his quest for Olympic gold.

It was against this backdrop that Glenn Morris, Jesse Owens and the rest of the American athletes departed for Germany. The team headed out of New York harbor on July 15, on the USS Manhattan, led by a small squadron of tugboats. The entire team consisted of 384 members, a record at that time, 66 of which were track-and-field athletes. Included were a pair of great sprinters – the spectacular Owens, who had set four world records in one day at the Big Ten Championships while starring for Ohio State, and Mack Robinson, whose kid brother Jackie would make sports history in baseball in 1947.

The athletes were provided a wide variety of activities to keep busy on the trip. Newsreel clips show the athletes playing shuffleboard and table tennis, and there were also friendly competitions. A masquerade party was held one night, and Brundage presented trophies to winners in several categories. In a poll of athletes, Mrs. Joanna DeTuscan, a fencer from Detroit, was the winner of a beauty contest, and track star Glenn Hardin of Louisiana was voted the most handsome man. When Hardin failed to show up in time to accept the prize, it was awarded to the man who placed second — Glenn Morris. Another Glenn, sprinter Cunningham, was voted the most popular athlete.

Marty Glickman was a member of the United States track team, and went on to a long and successful career as a national television sports announcer. He remembered Morris for his appearance and for his reserved manner.

"Glenn was perhaps the most handsome man on the whole team," said Glickman. "He had a lean, smoothly-muscled body, and hawk-like features, almost like an Indian.

"He was rather quiet, even aloof. He was not 'one of the boys,' if you know what

I mean. When we gathered, he was not usually one of the guys. The word 'respect' comes to mind, rather than well-liked. Others were more colorful; this was a serious, sober individual.

"But he was a great, great athlete," added Glickman. *(8)*

There were other diversions on the ship for the athletes besides innocent games. Holm, who had won a gold medal in swimming in the 1932 Olympics at age eighteen, was now a seasoned twenty-two, recently married, and anxious to have a good time on the long trip. She was seen sipping champagne and playing cards late at night, and a huge flap erupted. After the USS Manhattan docked, the U.S. Olympic Committee dismissed her from the team for what it termed misconduct, and the story was front-page news all over America. Not one to hold back, Holm leveled charges at the United States Olympic Committee.

"Militantly defending her own behavior, Eleanor charged officials 'disgraced' and 'misconducted' themselves on shipboard, and that at least 100 other athletes were guilty of infractions of training rules during the nine-day ocean voyage," reported the Associated Press from Berlin. Despite her protests, Holm was not reinstated, and wound up watching the Games from the stands. Decades later, Holm said she believed that Glenn Morris was among the athletes who had signed a petition requesting that she be dismissed for her actions on board ship.

There were other, more serious problems on the stormy Atlantic. The trip was cold and rainy, and many of the athletes fell ill. Morris was among that group, and couldn't work out regularly on the trip. A cold hit him hard, and as a result, he missed several key workouts. He gained weight and felt slow and sluggish. After nine days at seas, he arrived in Berlin in a less than optimistic mood.

"I gained about eight pounds going over," he wrote years later. "It rained most of the time and I hard a hard time losing the weight. I caught a cold which settled in my muscles, and I was too tensed up to work out for two days."

But once on dry land, he began to work out and recuperate quickly. By the start of competition, on August 7, Morris was almost back to peak strength. He had also moved into the favorite's role in the decathlon, as Hans Sievert withdrew from the competition with an injury. Morris expressed his feelings about the upcoming competition in a letter he wrote to George Whitman, sports chairman of the Denver Athletic Club.

"The people in Germany think a decathlon man is about tops in athletics, so I have been the target of autograph-seekers, movie cameras and the curious element. Hans Sievert has been over to see me and seemed surprised when I told him I was sorry he couldn't compete. I mean it. I wish he were competing so I can see if I really am the superior.

"I know I'll have some tough competition as it is, but I'm going to be ready….I'll not let you down if it's humanly possible to win. I'm going over 8,000 points or die.

"Max Schmeling came to the village yesterday and an Associated Press man had us doing some roadwork together for a picture."

A former heavyweight boxing champion of the world, Schmeling was the subject of hero worship all over Germany for his upset victory over the previously-undefeated Joe Louis on June 19 in Yankee Stadium. Louis had been considered unbeatable, but Schmeling knocked him out in the twelfth round. (On June 22, 1938, Louis got his revenge with a stunning first-round knockout of the German.)

Schmeling wasn't the only celebrity to visit the Olympic village. Among those who came by was Charles Lindbergh, who had become a sensation just nine years earlier with his solo flight of the Atlantic Ocean. At the request of photographers, Lindbergh jogged once around the practice track at the village, and later was pursued by Nazi leaders who desired to be seen in his company.

The impact of the Colorado comet on the Olympic scene even extended to the official program. A photo of Morris throwing the shot was selected to be on the cover. C.L. Parsons, sports editor of the Denver Post, wrote that the photo selection of Morris "just goes to show how Morris's feats have captured the minds of the fans and officials alike. I doubt if any athlete of the Rocky Mountain region ever left home with greater support and well wishes of his admirers."

Upon arriving in Berlin, the United States team had just two days to loosen up before the competition began. Coach Robertson directed Morris to spend some time on the shot put and the pole vault, even assigning the three members of the pole vault team to work with him. It was this event which concerned him the most, said the coach.

"He is a regular one-man track team," said Robertson of Morris. "He has been called 'the perfect athlete,' although this is not altogether true because he has one glaring weakness….the pole vault."

Morris received praise from another old-time coach, in a story that went national. Brutus Hamilton, age 86, was himself a former Olympic decathlon athlete and former head track coach at the University of California. He was a solid fan of the Colorado star.

"Hamilton…named Glenn Morris as the likeliest American winner in the Olympics," said the AP story. "Hamilton rates Morris as the most superb decathlon star of all time. 'Morris broke the world record but he has not yet reached his peak,' Hamilton said."

But the trip had taken a toll on Morris mentally as well as physically. Basically a loner since his youth, he made friends slowly. Carpenter, from the University of Southern California, was the athlete he hung out with the most. Glenn spent a lot of time by himself, undoubtedly contemplating the hours ahead and preparing for the coming showdown. He must have asked himself a hundred times how a kid from the plains of Colorado, from a town of less than six hundred people, could be in position to take on the greatest athletes from all over the world.

Usually optimistic before competition, Morris found his confidence faltering just a bit in the final twenty-four hours.

"The day before I began the decathlon, I was all alone in the village and consequently I was not relaxed when the final call was sounded," he said later.

Besides the competition itself, and the overwhelming stadium and large crowds, the athletes were exposed to the spectacle of Hitler arriving on a daily basis, amid tremendous fanfare. It left a profound impression on most of them, including Jesse

Owens.

"I remember seeing Hitler coming in with his entourage and the storm troopers standing shoulder-to-shoulder like an iron fence," Owens said years later. "Then came the roar of 'Heil Hitler' from 100,000 throats. It was eerie and frightening." *(9)*

Less frightening, of course, was the presence of Leni Riefenstahl's crew of workers and photographers. They were ubiquitous, determined to take film from every conceivable angle. In her own way, she was as obsessed with her mission as Morris was with his.

"Leni Riefenstahl's cinema photographers were all over Berlin...." reported Richard D. Mandell in his book, *The Nazi Olympics*. "They were lodged in the hovering Zeppelins, atop towers, and in pits at all the competitions." *(10)*

When the decathlon began on August 7, there were twenty-eight competitors on hand, representing seventeen different nations. Morris got off to a slow start, while his teammate, Bob Clark, blasted into the lead. In the first event, Clark turned in a blazing 10.9 in the 100-meter sprint, while Morris finished in 11.1 seconds. In the second event, Clark took the broad jump competition with a superb leap of 25 feet even, while Morris finished second at 23 feet, 10 and one-half inches.

The third event was the shot put, and here Morris's power showed itself. He won the competition with a heave of 46 feet and two and one-half inches, far ahead of Clark. Morris roared back with a high jump of six feet, two inches – good for second place behind Reindert Brasser of Holland. The day's fifth and final event was the 400-meter run. Morris turned in a sensational 49.4-second effort to finish ahead of the field. At day's end, the two Americans led the standings, and the Coloradan was only two points behind Clark, with 4,192 points. But there was some disturbing news waiting for Morris.

"There was no preparation made for feeding the athletes at the stadium on Friday, and the Olympic Village was ten miles away," Glenn said later. "I drank four cups of coffee and ate a steak sandwich at noon Friday. I am not used to drinking coffee during the day and slept only two hours Friday night.

"However, I felt fairly well rested Saturday morning...."

Saturday, August 8, was drizzly and cool. On the first day, Morris had spent his time pacing nervously in the practice area. On the second day, he and Clark shared a ritual between events. They found a quiet spot in the stadium and spread a blanket on the ground, then draped a towel over their heads. On occasion, Morris would even roll up in the blanket in an attempt to keep his body warm. He was preparing himself mentally for the pinnacle of his entire life. He was determined to make the folks back home proud and happy, and to also vanquish the obsessive drive gnawing inside of him. Only a gold medal would satisfy both urges.

Saturday's first event must have reminded him of his early days back in Simla, where he had devoted countless hours leaping makeshift hurdles put up by his older cousin and neighbor, Bill Moreland. He had always loved the hurdles, and he showed the Berlin crowd why. He won the 110-meter hurdles in 14.9 seconds, compared to a 15.7 clocking by Clark....and moved into first place. Suddenly, he was oblivious to the weather and all else as he zeroed in on his goal.

The seventh event was the discus, and Morris began to pull away. He captured first with a heave of 141 feet, four inches, while Clark recorded a mere 129 feet, two inches. Clark tightened the race considerably with his 12-foot, one-and 11/16ths-inch effort in the pole vault, without question Morris's weakest event. The best Glenn could muster was an 11-foot, five-and-13/16s inch vault, which placed him in the middle of the pack.

All during the final day's events, Morris was the subject of great attention. Most of the fans – and Leni's film crew – were watching his every move in the stadium, even in the practice area.

"Throughout the competition Friday and Saturday, Morris held the attention of the crowd whether he was competing or waiting for the next event," declared the Denver Post. "Throughout the long grind, Morris scarcely ever rested. When he wasn't competing, he usually went off by himself at one end of the field and practiced alone for the next event." It seems, the Post reporters must not have noticed his habit of covering up with a blanket.

The javelin throw, much more popular in Europe than the United States, was the ninth event. The winner was Edvard Natvig of Norway, with a heave of 190 feet, six inches. Morris only managed to place ninth with an effort of 178 feet, 10 and ½ inches....but it was still far better than Clark, who was more than 11 feet behind Morris. With just one event left, the Colorado comet held a slim advantage.

A Hitler youth demonstration held up the final event, the 1,500-meter run, for almost ninety minutes. And to complicate matters further, it was incorrectly announced that in order for Morris to set a new world record, he would have to run the 1,500 in 4:32 – a time he had never achieved. But the delay only strengthened his resolve. Nearly ten hours after the first event began on Saturday, the tenth and final event began.

It was to be Glenn's finest moment.

He "poured everything into the race," wrote a Denver reporter. "During the second lap a Belgian runner cut in front of him, bringing the throng of 90,000 to their feet in a hail of boos. Morris regained the lead. Der Fuhrer cheered the American on. Morris won in his fastest time ever, 4:33.3, then collapsed in a heap, convinced that his effort had not been good enough.

"A hush fell over the crowd. Morris got up, then heard the loudspeaker crack. There had been a gross misstatement. The 4:32 mark had only been an estimate. Glenn Morris had completed the best decathlon in history and had scored 7,900 points!"

"Those last forty yards were torturous," wrote famed sportswriter Arthur J. Daley of The New York Times, describing Morris's courageous finish. "His features were strained and drawn. Every step was painful, but still he came on, running only with his heart. His feet were leaden."

"That race was one of the dramatic peaks of the Olympics," wrote Mandell in *The Nazi Olympics*. "Morris was already played out. His gait was graceless and as he forced his energies, his pensive face was torn with anguish." *(11)*

It had been a marvelous showing and Morris's efforts had dazzled the crowd.

"The Colorado boy even had Hitler excitedly rocking back and forth like a coxswain coaxing a crew as he led the throng of 90,000 in cheering the American down the stretch in the 1,500 meters," wrote the Denver Post in its August 9 issue. "Hitler, who usually leaves before darkness, remained Saturday until 8:19 to watch Morris complete the most remarkable exhibition of athletic prowess ever displayed by a human being. As Morris battled during the final few yards of the 1,500 meters, Hitler pounded his fist into a cupped hand, obviously excited over the American's courageous finish."

It was over. The young man from Simla was now officially declared the greatest athlete in the entire world! En route to his gold medal, Morris had won five of the ten events – the 110-meter hurdles, the discus throw, the shot put, the 400 meters and the 1,500 meters. It was a stunning blend of power and speed that had propelled him to the top....with a tremendous dosage of pure guts tossed in for good measure.

"Morris literally ran himself into exhaustion and into the record books with yet another world record," reported Zarnowski decades later. *(12)* It was an American sweep as Clark earned the silver medal and Jack Parker won the bronze.

Glenn received his laurel wreath from Eva Braun, Hitler's mistress. The same age as Morris, Eva had been Hitler's constant companion for nearly four years, and was apparently enthralled by Morris's performance. "The blonde, fresh-faced, slim, photographer's assistant was an athletic girl, fond of skiing, mountain climbing and gymnastics, as well as dancing." *(13)* With her interest in athletics and physiques, the Olympics would have been very exciting for her, and she very likely could have developed an infatuation for the handsome athlete from America.

Morris was the star attraction, along with Owens, for the remainder of the Olympics. Now, he suddenly had time to spend some time with the stunning woman who had been taking film of him for two days, and it seemed Leni could hardly wait.

By the time the Olympics hit Berlin, Leni Riefenstahl may have been the most famous woman in the country. Born on August 22, 1902, she was ten years older than Morris. In her youth she studied painting and ballet and began her professional career as a dancer. She took up acting in the late 1920s and forged a very successful career, based on her stunning good looks and talent for the dramatic. But, wanting more control of projects she was passionate about, she turned to directing in 1931 and formed her own film company. Somewhere about that time she met Adolph Hitler, and subsequently she made several documentaries which promoted the values of physical beauty and Aryan superiority. Her work was praised for its combination of rich musical scores, cinematic beauty and brilliant editing. It was that reputation and her relationship with the most powerful man in Germany that allowed her to have such free rein at the 1936 Olympics.

Just what transpired over the next ten days is hard to confirm. The most intriguing account came from Riefenstahl herself, nearly sixty years later in her memoirs. The book, published in 1994 by St. Martin's Press, offers a no-holds-barred look at the world of the legendary filmmaker. Just how much of it is true would be impossible to ascertain, but the picture Leni draws of her relationship with Glenn Morris is both absorbing and disturbing.

According to Riefenstahl, she was given an introduction to all three American decathlon stars by Erwin Huber, a good friend of hers who was in the event.

"With a towel over his head, Glenn Morris lay relaxing on the grass, gathering strength for the next event. When Huber presented Morris to me, and we looked at one another, we both seemed transfixed. It was an incredible moment and I had never experienced anything like it," she confessed in her memoirs. *(14)*

Neither, apparently, had Morris. Judging by his alleged actions over the next week, and by statements made to his brother years later, the meeting with Riefenstahl would impact his life greatly and haunt him for decades. It certainly had a powerful effect on Leni: "I tried to choke back the feelings surging up inside me and to forget what had happened. From then on, I avoided Morris, with whom I exchanged barely a dozen words, and yet this meeting had had a profound impact on me."

The meeting had been innocent enough, and she had surely seen Morris prior to meeting him officially. And there was much more to come, according to Leni. She ran into the American star shortly after the medal presentation, while both were still in the stadium. She wrote in her memoirs that when she offered to shake his hand in congratulations, he grabbed her and kissed her so wildly that her blouse was nearly torn off "in front of a hundred thousand spectators." (15)

The plot thickened when she discovered back in her lab that darkness had prevented her from getting adequate footage from the pole vault finals. She went to Huber to see if he could get the medal-winning pole vaulters to come back to the stadium the next day and have them recreate that event in the stadium.

The Americans had left the Olympic village and were at a nightclub. Huber told her that only Glenn Morris could get them to come back and help her, and that Morris had agreed to do it....if she would allow him to visit her editing room to see the film she had taken of him. She reluctantly agreed: "I gave in to his request but otherwise avoided him," she wrote, " for I sensed that I was in love with him and must struggle against it. I knew he would be returning to the United States, and besides, I wanted to resist any emotional complications." *(16)*

Far from avoiding complications, the involvement between the two world-famous figures apparently exploded. It happened after Riefenstahl discovered that the film she had taken of the decathlon's 1,500-meter run was also no good. She decided to re-shoot that event, too; both Huber and the Czech runner were still in Berlin, but Morris had gone with the American team to Stockholm. Following the close of the Olympics, American athletes were in high demand by various European countries and a number of tours were set up by the U.S. Olympic Committee.

"The success of the American track and field athletes increased the desire of foreign countries to have the outstanding stars appear in their athletic centers," wrote Daniel Ferris of the U.S. Olympic Committee. "All countries wanted Owens, Cunningham, Woodruff, Williams, Morris, Towns, Johnson and men of that calibre." *(17)*

Riefenstahl's people contacted Morris, and he agreed to come back to Berlin for a re-shoot.

"When we picked Morris up at the airport, we both had to behave so that no one would notice anything," wrote Leni. "But we couldn't control our feelings. They were so powerful that Morris did not rejoin his team in Sweden, and I imagined that he was the man I would marry." *(18)*

One can easily picture the passion between the two in Leni's apartment. They were two highly-charged personalities who were poised at the top of the world in terms of fame and glory. The attraction they felt for each other was obviously incredible. "I had lost my head completely. I forgot almost everything, even my work," she wrote. "Never before had I experienced such a passion." *(19)*

With one night left before the American team left Hamburg for America, Leni managed to talk Morris into leaving her apartment with her and returning to the stadium to reshoot the climactic scene of the 1,500-meter run. Her crew hurried to the stadium and was able to get the footage she wanted for the documentary. They wrapped up after midnight, and Leni claims that she and Morris returned to her apartment.

"When Morris had to leave me at the crack of dawn, a sense of great sadness overwhelmed us," she reported.

The romantic, clandestine relationship between the two is doubted by some, but it seems that for Riefenstahl to make up a fictional account some sixty years later would serve no purpose whatsoever. It certainly does nothing to enhance her standing on the world stage or to improve her reputation as a femme fatale. She wrote that she was shocked to find out from the press that Morris was engaged to an American woman and she admitted "it took me six months to get over Glenn Morris."

One is hard pressed indeed to see what her motivation would be to make up such a tale six decades later. In addition, her story is given degrees of credibility by four other sources.

First, some decathletes in latter years reportedly were familiar with the possible romance between the two: "I was first told of the affair by a Swedish decathlete years later," said Frank Zarnowski, the author of the book *The Decathlon*. "We were sitting in the stands watching a decathlon when he started talking about Glenn Morris and Leni Riefenstahl. He acted like it was fairly well known in some European track circles."

Secondly, Carpenter, who won the gold medal in the discus, also alluded to an obvious affection between them: "Glenn Morris was a good friend of mine," said Carpenter, when talking to author Lewis Carlson in 1980. "Leni took a liking to Glenn, and myself. Glenn almost had Leni talked into having dinner with Hitler one night." *(20)*

Third, Sparks Alfred, a man who knew Morris well and acted as a father figure to him during Alfred's days as a trainer at Colorado State College, spoke of it: "I went to Fort Collins and visited with Sparks shortly before his death," said Morris Ververs in 2000. A former principal at Simla High School, Ververs has devoted considerable time and effort to tracing the career of Glenn Morris.

"Sparks told me that Glenn had come to see him shortly after returning from Berlin. He told him some stories that Sparks had never confided to anyone else, until talking with me. There were some wild stories, and they involved Glenn and Leni

**Glenn Morris as a member of the Denver Athletic Club,
just prior to his departure for Berlin.**

Glenn Morris

**The streets of Berlin were filled with enthusiastic fans....and Olympic signs
mingled with Nazi banners to create a strange image.**

In an incredible scene, the airship Hindenberg floats over the massive monument leading into Berlin, with the Nazi flags and Olympic flags flying side by side. Nine months later, on May 6, 1937, the Hindenberg exploded over Lakehurst, New Jersey, in one of the worst aviation accidents ever.

Glenn worked on his sprinting techniques while on the nine-day ocean voyage to Berlin.

Remembers Girl He Left Behind Him
Associated Press Wirephoto

ABOVE: in the August 2, 1936 issue of the Denver Post, Glenn is pictured aboard ship writing a letter to Charlotte Edwards back in Fort Collins.

LEFT: Glenn goes for a jog in the Olympic Village with former world heavyweight boxing champion Max Schmeling (center) and USA teammate Walter Wood, a discus thrower. (*AP Photo*)

The American team parades around the stadium in Berlin at the opening day of the 1936 Olympics.

Chancellor Hitler and his Nazi officials give the "Heil Hitler" salute prior to the start of the 1936 Olympics in Berlin.

LEFT: Leni Riefenstahl enjoys some moments with Adolph Hitler.

BOTTOM: Leni works with her camera crew in Berlin.

LEFT: Leni Riefenstahl as an actress in 1930.

Glenn warms up on the
hurdle, stretches
in the grass, walks on
his hands and gets in
some pole vaulting
practice prior to the start
of the Games
in Berlin.

**First and foremost, Glenn Morris was a runner, at any distance or with
hurdles in front of him. From his youth in Simla up through college
days at Colorado State, and in the Olympics, running was his forte.
Here he is shown in two races at the Olympic Games in Berlin.**

The decathlon takes a
variety of athletic skills,
as Morris shows here
in the 1936 Olympics.
He is pictured in the
long jump (top left),
the pole vault (top),
the hurdles (center)
and the shot put (left).

LEFT: Three American flags fly over the scoreboard, showing the top three placewinners in the grueling decathlon.

ZEHNKAMPF			
MORRIS	U S A	7900	P
CLARK	U S A	7601	P
PARKER	U S A	7275	P
HUBER	DEUTSCHLAND	7087	P
BRASSER	HOLLAND	7046	P
GUHL	SCHWEIZ	7033	P

BELOW: The stadium was packed every day during the track and field events, often with crowds of 90,000.

LEFT: Eva Braun, mistress of German Chancellor Adolph Hitler, gives the laurel wreath to Glenn.

BELOW: Glenn and his two teammates pose on the awards stand as the National Anthem is played.

BELOW: Glenn signs autographs for some young German fans.

The photos on this page show
Glenn during the filming of the
documentary *Olympiad*,
except for the bottom photo
where Glenn takes a break
between events during
the actual competition.

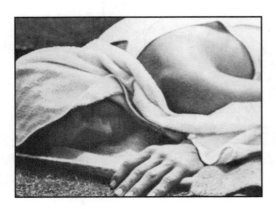

TOP: In a stunning photo from the National Archives, Leni Riefenstahl brushes back the hair on Glenn's face after the completion of the decathlon competition. Off Glenn's right shoulder is Jack Parker, who won the bronze medal in the decathlon.

BOTTOM: Leni's camera crew shoots Glenn throwing the discus.

LEFT: Jesse Owens was the biggest star of the 1936 Olympics, running away with four gold medals.

BELOW: Ken Carpenter, probably Glenn's closest friend on the Olympic team, won the gold medal in the discus event.

He Lives Up to His Boast

GLENN MORRIS,

Before he sailed for the Berlin Olympics games, Glenn Morris, Colorado State College, boasted that he would break decathlon record. He made good today by smashing the decathlon record in the 110-meter hurdles and winning the discus to take the decathlon championship at Berlin.

I'LL BREAK IT INTO A THOUSAND PIECES

THE OLD RECORD

LEFT: His tremendous victory in the decathlon made Glenn a popular figure with sports writers and cartoonists all across the nation.

Glenn is a study in concentration as he prepares for a javelin throw in Berlin. His ability to focus in and concentrate on each event was one of Glenn's biggest assets as an athlete.

The javelin is one of the most beautiful events of the decathlon, but was not one of Glenn's best events because it is much more popular in Europe than in the United States.

(Left photo by Leni Riefenstahl)

Getting ready to board a plane for a public appearance were Olympic stars Glenn Cunningham (left), who won a silver medal in the 1500 meters; Glenn (center) and Earl Meadows, who won a gold medal in the pole vault.

Three famous Colorado athletes got together in 1940 for a banquet in Denver. They are (from left) Glenn Morris, Earl "Dutch" Clark, and Byron "Whizzer" White, who later became a U.S. Supreme Court Justice.

Winning the Olympics made Glenn Morris big news all over the world. He was the main story on the Denver sports page (top left), and made the cover of a popular German magazine (left). On Glenn Morris Day, he held his gold medal for the camera (above).

Glenn Morris Day in Denver attracted over 10,000 fans to honor the state's "overnight" sensation. This photo appeared in the Denver Post on September 9, 1936. Glenn is in the front car at the bottom of the page.

(Photo courtesy of the Denver Post)

Glenn Morris Visits Old Home Town

**TOP: This photo appeared in the Denver Post the day after Glenn Morris Day, with the following cutline:
Glenn Morris (right), Colorado Olympic decathlon champion, ready to hop off byplane Saturday with pilot A.A. Sherred for his birthplace at Simla, where a big hometown celebration was held in his honor.**

LEFT: The AAU voted the 1936 Sullivan Award to Glenn, as the top amateur athlete in the entire United States.

**Charlotte and Glenn were the two most popular
citizens in Colorado on Glenn Morris Day in Denver,
when some 10,000 people came to see them.**

(Denver Post photo)

Riefenstahl."

In 1996, freelance writer Stephen L. Harris, writing for *The Burroughs Bulletin*, stated that he was confident the affair took place. In an article entitled "Olympic Love Affair," Harris writes that the two were caught up in a passion that would not be denied. "Her march across the infield stirred Morris," wrote Harris. "His sweetheart back home was a beauty. Without her help, he knew he'd have been elsewhere that moment instead of at the Olympics. But the gorgeous German now before him swept away in a heartbeat whatever feelings he held for Charlotte."

Finally, the relationship was commented on by Morris himself near the end of his life. Jack Morris said his brother referred to Leni in a very wistful manner one of the last times he saw him alive. The affair with this dazzling woman was to have a profound affect on Morris, perhaps even causing the breakup of his first marriage and fueling his determination to find a glamorous spot in the world in the years ahead. Perhaps the unfulfilled love he felt for this German beauty left him desperately seeking a romance that would never be realized, all the rest of his life.

At least two people who have considerable knowledge of the 1936 Olympics dispute the notion that Riefenstahl and Morris had an affair.

"I never heard a whisper of it," said Mandell. "Riefenstahl lied about everything that occurred to her during the Nazi regime. She was sexually ruthless, a sexual predator." *(21)*

Eleanor Holm, who co-starred with Morris two years later in "Tarzan's Revenge," also finds the story hard to swallow.

"That's ridiculous," she said, about the account in the Riefenstahl book. "As far as I was concerned, Morris was a dull country boy. If he would have attacked Riefenstahl in the stadium like she says, it would have made big headlines all over the world. Look what happened to me for just sipping champagne.

"In addition, I can vouch for the made-up stories that were bandied about. It was said in the papers that I had gone to parties with (Hermann) Goring and swam naked at the parties. That's just a bunch of crap. I never did that." *(22)*

Harold E. "Rusty" Wilson, who owns a doctorate in sports history studies from Ohio State University, has spent considerable time researching the Olympic Games in general, and the 1936 Olympics in particular. He has interviewed many medal winners from the Berlin Games, and feels the story of the affair has strong elements of truth to it. But he also doubts some of the details.

"From what I know, I think something happened between them," Wilson said in a 2002 phone interview. "However, I think it was exaggerated by Leni; I think she basically over-dramatized everything, particularly the part about attacking her at the awards ceremony. Some of the athletes who were there and actually saw Morris receive his gold medal told me they didn't see anything like that at all. They said he basically took his gold medal, smiled and walked quietly away, shy and kind of sheepish. They said that was not the type of guy he was (to go after Leni in front of the crowd), that he wouldn't flaunt it. They don't doubt that something happened between them, because that sort of thing (between athletes and German women) was going on all over the place."

On October 15, 2002, Riefenstahl, in her 100th year, responded to a letter asking about the comments in her memoirs, and the doubts expressed by Holm and Mandell.

She explained there were no pictures taken at the time because "it was simply too dark (and) we couldn't even shoot the winner's laurel. You will not find it in the movie either, because not one meter of film or photos are existing. You can be sure that all I told in my memoirs corresponds to the truth 100 percent." *(23)*

It was also obvious from the letter, written sixty-six years after the Berlin Olympics had closed, that Leni Riefenstahl had not erased memories of Glenn Morris from her mind: "Your letter....was very moving," she wrote to the author. "The recollection of the times I spent with Glenn up to the sad ending is still very strong."

What happened between Leni Riefenstahl and Glenn Morris prior to his leaving Berlin may never be authenticated. But various rumors persist. Another story suggested that Eva Braun was also infatuated with Glenn, and tried to arrange a meeting with him. A third story revolves around a fantastic offer that may have come from The Fuhrer himself.

It was widely known that Hitler was very enthusiastic about Morris's performance in the decathlon. There seems little doubt that Hitler and his propaganda minister, Joseph Goebbels, would have seen some benefit in having "the world's greatest athlete" stay behind in Berlin and be put to use in some fashion that would show German superiority in a dramatic fashion.

"It was further reported that Glenn was offered $50,000 to stay in Germany and make sports movies, an offer that he declined," wrote Fred W. Smith in an article about Morris which appeared in a Tarzan fan magazine after his death in 1974. "It makes me wonder if Hitler was seeing his dream of a superman in Glenn Morris." In 2001, Glenn's sister, Virginia Morris Baxter, said that Glenn had actually told her of an offer made by the Germans, but she did not know any of the details.

If Riefenstahl's stories are true, Morris undoubtedly faced the long journey home by ship with very mixed, perhaps even torturous, feelings. He wrote to his brother, Jack, the day the team was to depart. The letter offers a glimpse into his mood, and into what he had experienced in his incredible trip overseas:

"It gave me a thrill to see this beautiful ship pull up and dock at Southhampton. It had been nearly two weeks since I had seen some of the fellows, so you can imagine how good it was to see them again.

"Everybody aboard has been treating me like a king. In fact, they call me the king of athletes. Could you ever imagine this coming true? Neither could I. Hope the folks and all of you are as happy as I am. I'll be staying in New York for four days to talk business with some fellows.

"I have many, many experiences to tell you," he wrote, adding he preferred to tell them to Jack in person rather than via the mail. Reading the letter some six decades after it was written, it seems obvious that Glenn was reaching out for acceptance to his family in general, and to his older brother in particular. He was indeed proud of all that he had accomplished, and rightfully so. But there is a certain tentativeness that comes through.

"Be happy and write me soon at the Denver Athletic Club," Glenn concluded.

Morris returned to a huge welcome in the United States. He was honored, along with Jesse Owens and other Olympic stars, at a ticker-tape parade in New York City. He was even given the center seat in the lead auto by Mayor Fiorello LeGuardia. Then, it was on to Colorado for a large parade in Denver, where Governor Ed Johnson issued a "Glenn Morris Day" proclamation for September 6. "I'm thrilled to be back in Colorado with my old friends," Glenn told a Denver Post sportswriter. "Although my great adventure in winning the decathlon in the Olympic Games was a great thrill, I can't tell you how happy I am to be home."

There was also an exhibition at Denver stadium, with an estimated 10,000 fans in attendance. Glenn showed the huge crowd some of the skills that had earned him the title "world's greatest athlete." A front-page story in the Denver Post declared him to be one of the biggest heroes in the history of the state.

"Glenn Morris, Olympic decathlon champion, returned to his home in Fort Collins Thursday with the cheers of thousands ringing in his ears, a testimonial to the finest and most spontaneous tribute ever paid by Colorado to one of her native sons," declared the article in the Post.

"An all-day celebration of his homecoming from Berlin – starting with a parade thru (sic) the business section and an official demonstration at Denver Stadium attended by 10,000 – reached a climax Wednesday night when a distinguished gathering of city and state officials and business and professional leaders added their cheers to a banquet at the Denver Athletic Club." (September 10, 1936 edition). Some of the event was even broadcast nationally by NBC radio.

Writer Ralph Radetsky paid further homage on the inside pages of the Post.

"….for the first time in the history of the city the voice of all the people was raised in tribute to 'a faultless body and a blameless mind' Denver has seen many parades for many reasons. There was never a parade similar to that which did honor to the world's greatest all-around athlete…."

Charlotte was flown in from Fountain, where she was working as a teacher, and posed proudly by Glenn's side for photographers.

Governor Johnson ordered the capitol building closed at noon, and requested that schools and service clubs urge people to attend. His proclamation, read before the huge crowd, went as follows: "A modest, courteous, gentlemanly fellow, with a trained and educated mind housed in a clean, strong, healthy body – that is Glenn Morris. He represents the very objective in human development that we are striving to attain in Colorado. It requires planning, great patience and faith; it requires hard work and determination to produce that sort of a human being.

"We are justly proud of his marvelous feat and his phenomenal achievement, and we want to show our keen interest in his accomplishments and great appreciation to him personally by publicly celebrating his victory."

Not to be outdone, Simla planned its own celebration, scheduled for Saturday, September 12. Nearly 3,000 fans showed up, along with Mayor J.C. Schuster, and former schoolmates, to honor him. "WELCOME HOME" blared the headline in The Simla Sun, sporting a large photo of Glenn in a sport coat and holding a shot, a javelin and a pole.

"A free barbecue 'Bigger and Better' than ever, with 2,500 pounds of beef and everything that goes with it, entertainment for all and a program to keep you busy all day long, climaxed by a 'Welcome Home Dance' at night, have been planned for this greatest celebration in Simla history," said the story in the Simla Sun. Glenn and the governor were flown in from Denver on a special flight for the occasion.

The school district also planned a dinner in his honor. Signs proclaiming that Simla was the hometown of the world's greatest athlete, each with a picture of Glenn, were erected on the entrance to town on Highway 24. The Colorado State College campus was presented an oak tree by Glenn, to be planted in a special area. All Olympic champions were given a potted oak tree by the German hosts to be brought back to their native land, as an enduring symbol of their victories. Both Denver and Simla had expressed strong interest in the tree, but Glenn opted for the Fort Collins campus where he had trained so long and hard to become the best in the world.

The honors didn't end in Colorado, either. Though the fabled Jesse Owens won four gold medals and set three world records in the Berlin Olympics, Morris was voted the James E. Sullivan Award by the AAU as the nation's outstanding athlete of 1936. Not wanting to be left out, the Detroit Lions of the National Football League extended a contract and invited him to their camp.

"Cheering thousands wildly acclaim Glenn Morris on return home," blared a headline in the Rocky Mountain News of Denver on September 10, 1936. Underneath the headline were four large photos of Glenn, and a column by Chet Nelson, sports editor of the Rocky Mountain News.

"Yes, Glenn Morris can take it," wrote Nelson. "He has been one of the most entertained individuals in the world the last month. But Glenn Morris hasn't changed. At least, I couldn't see any change in the several hours I was around him Wednesday. And I am sure the thousands of admirers who gave him such a rousing welcome will agree with my observations."

Yet, there were some storm clouds starting to form on faraway horizons. By virtue of his sensational performance in Berlin, Morris had become the toast of the athletic world. But even amid the incredible glory and fanfare, there was something gnawing at him. According to his brother, Jack, he was disappointed that no one from his family was able to make the trip to Germany to see him at his finest hour, or to see him in Denver and Simla.

"Everybody was so proud of him. I was working in the mines in Ward, Colorado," said Jack decades later. "I had been school teaching, but gave it up for the mines because I could make so much more money.

"The Olympics and all was kind of sad in a way, though, because he expected the family to do more, to be there, I guess. But we had no money. Going to Berlin was totally out of the question for mom and dad, or any of us. And we couldn't be in New York for the big parade, or any of that. Glenn wanted us there, to share in it all. We couldn't, and that always seemed to bother him.

"He always felt, to a degree, that the family – the parents, mostly – never did enough for him, that they somehow let him down. That's sad."

In fact, John and Emma had moved from Simla to the state of Washington in 1935 — "they had always wanted to be around fruit trees," said their daughter, Virginia Baxter, in 2001. "We weren't able to participate in any of the activities in Simla or Denver. I was just a young girl then and was worried about other things, like the big move. But now I wish I could have been there and been a part of it all."

There seems little doubt that Glenn was also being pulled in two different directions by his romantic inclinations for two completely different types of women. Although Charlotte and Leni had a common beauty, they were as different as any two women could possibly be in their backgrounds, temperaments and viewpoints of life. Charlotte was a quiet and modest schoolteacher in Colorado, while Leni was a top celebrity and the toast of Germany and much of Europe. Glenn Morris would soon have to choose between the two, whether he wanted to or not.

While there was much to be sorted out and dealt with, there was also adulation; tons of it, pouring in from every corner of America. Though he accepted a job as a radio announcer with NBC in New York, Glenn stayed only a brief time, hoping to find something even more lucrative. He was offered opportunities to endorse a wide range of products, ranging from suits to watches to a breakfast food. His sister, Virginia, said he turned most of them down, perhaps in an attempt to save his amateur status in case he wanted to compete further in track. From New York City to Denver, Glenn Morris became the toast of America. And his fame spread even to the West Coast, where the movie kingdom was taking notice.

On To Hollywood

The day before the Olympics began, the Associated Press ran a photo of a smiling Glenn Morris sitting at his desk in the Olympic village, writing a letter to Charlotte Edwards. The caption read "Remembers Girl He Left Behind Him." Glenn was wearing an USA sweater, and had a photo of Charlotte sitting on his desk. During a radio interview, he apparently proposed to Charlotte....from Berlin. But there is some controversy about the proposal. His sister, Virginia Baxter, said Glenn denied proposing but insisted that he was set up by a question from the radio interviewer which suggested he was engaged to Charlotte. "He felt trapped" by that radio interview, Virginia said more than six decades later. Ironically, the radio interview came the day before he met Leni Riefenstahl.

Charlotte was at Glenn's side for the post-Olympic celebration in Denver, and was the subject of a long story in the Denver Post: "....her voice almost a whisper from nervousness, (she) did not look the triumphant fiancée of the nation's greatest athlete, but instead she looked the charming teacher she is and is going to be." When the interviewer asked Glenn about his plans, and he mentioned Hollywood, Charlotte was asked to respond.

"I wouldn't presume to tell Glenn what to do, or not to do," she said. "I couldn't express an opinion on whether or not I would like Hollywood as I know so little about it." The name of Leni Riefenstahl appeared in the same story, as Glenn explained she had taken photos of him for her documentary. He even produced an album of photos of himself, taken by Leni. He had sent some of the photos to Hollywood at the request of Sol Lesser, a producer who was planning a new Tarzan movie.

Leni's documentary was supported by a huge book entitled *Beauty in the Olympic Struggle*. She wrote the preface herself, describing the experience in glowing terms. It is very interesting, and perhaps insightful, to note that the very first athlete she mentions in the preface is the star from Simla:

"The Olympics — festival of youth, festival of beauty. Seldom has there been so much beauty combined with grace and strength as in those sixteen days of the Olympic Games in Berlin. Everything was beautiful: the Olympic idea, the torchbearer, the stadium — and the athletes: the rapture of Glenn Morris, the stride of Jesse Owens, the controlled power of our Karl Hein..."

Back in the States, Glenn was struggling emotionally to keep pace with all that was happening to him. Almost overnight, he had become the pride of Colorado, and one of the two brightest stars of the American team — the other being, of course, the incomparable Owens.

Regardless of his feelings for Leni, the relationship between Glenn and Charlotte was on a train that was nearly impossible to stop. They were married on December 13, 1936, in her hometown of Sterling, about ninety miles straight east of Fort Collins. Her father was the chief chemist at the Great Western Sugar Company in Sterling and the family was prosperous. Serving as best man was Harry Hughes, Glenn's football and track coach at Colorado A&M. The wedding was big enough national news that it was mentioned in *Newsweek* magazine.

Shortly after the ceremony, the new husband and wife team departed for California. Glenn had received word he had been selected by Lesser to become the ninth actor to play Tarzan. He was riding high on a crest, and could hardly imagine anything going afoul. After all, his incredible work ethic and optimism had held him in good stead for all of his twenty-five years to date. He and Charlotte found a cottage in Tarzana, a suburb of Los Angeles. The sprawling city was named after the fictional apeman when author Edgar Rice Burroughs moved from Chicago and purchased a huge ranch.

Tarzan was an early-American success story of immense proportions. Long before the debut of costumed heroes such as Superman and Batman, and even prior to Mickey Mouse arriving on the scene, Tarzan was a household name. The first Tarzan book, *Tarzan of the Apes*, was published in 1914. Four years later, barrel-chested Elmo Lincoln made the first Tarzan film. It was a smash success, and the film debut made author Edgar Rice Burroughs one of the hottest properties in Hollywood. Burroughs moved to the San Fernando Valley, and founded the community that eventually became known as Tarzana.

Gene Polar, a New York fireman; P. Dempsey Tabler, a former opera singer, and James Pierce, a former Indiana University football player, all made Tarzan movies in the 1920s. The first great athlete to play the role was muscular Frank Merrill, who had developed a tremendous physique while winning regional and national titles in gymnastics. Merrill invented the tree swinging routine (the other film Tarzans merely leaped from branch to branch) and also uttered the first Tarzan yell.

In 1931, producer William Van Dyke, feeling Merrill was too old, began the search for a new Tarzan. "I want someone like Jack Dempsey, only younger," said Van Dyke. Dempsey, at age thirty-seven in 1931, was one of the great athletic stars of the Roaring '20s, and had retired from boxing by then.

Herman Brix, who played three years of football at the University of Washington and won a total of six national titles in the shot put, became his choice. In the 1928 Olympics in Amsterdam, Brix earned the silver medal, and wound up in Los Angeles, training for the 1932 Olympics. Film star Douglas Fairbanks befriended him and when Fairbanks heard Van Dyke was looking for a new Tarzan, he sent Brix over for an audition.

After winning the Tarzan role, Brix still had to fulfill a previous commitment for a small role in a football movie called "Touchdown." Though never injured in three years of varsity football at Washington, he fell and broke his shoulder on the movie set. Too anxious to get started with his Tarzan project to wait for the shoulder to heal, Van Dyke signed another Olympic star, swimmer Johnny Weissmuller, for the role.

Weissmuller learned to swim on the shores of Lake Michigan, in Chicago. He developed his lean body into the perfect swimming machine, and became the talk of the sporting world. He won three gold medals at the 1924 Olympics in Paris, and two more in Amsterdam. Ironically, Weissmuller, Brix and Buster Crabbe were Olympic teammates in 1928. Weissmuller was teamed with a young, beautiful Irish actress named Maureen O'Sullivan, and the two of them made box office magic. "Tarzan, the Apeman," was one of the top ten hits of 1932, grossing several million dollars.

In 1933, Lesser decided to tap into the successful formula and bought the rights for one Tarzan movie. For the lead, he selected Crabbe, who won a bronze medal in 1928 in the 1,500-meter freestyle event and a gold medal in 1932 in the 400-meter freestyle. The film, "Tarzan the Fearless," continued to portray Tarzan as a simpleton in the MGM fashion made popular by Weissmuller.

Frustrated, Burroughs formed his own film company in 1935 and set off for the jungles of Guatemala, with Herman Brix as his Tarzan. The company produced two films; first came a serial entitled "The New Adventures of Tarzan." The second film was a full feature entitled "Tarzan and the Green Goddess." Brix played Tarzan as intelligent and articulate. Leaner and more muscular than either Weissmuller or Crabbe, Brix brought a fresh look and a new dignity to the role. But MGM, which had strong connections with movie theatre owners across the land, threatened to boycott theatres that showed the Burroughs film, and the movie had a very limited screening in America.

By 1937, Lesser was planning another try at Tarzan. Working with author Burroughs, he secured the rights for five more Tarzan films, and a series of other films based on stories written by the prolific author. The list of candidates for the Tarzan role was long and impressive. Among the stars apparently being considered were New York Yankees baseball hero Lou Gehrig, Yale football star Larry Kelly, boxing champions Max Baer and Jimmy Braddock, and professional wrestlers Sandor Szabo and Dave Levin.

There was a large number of news articles across the nation discussing the possibilities of Gehrig, the game's premier power hitter with the decline of Babe Ruth, as the next Tarzan. He was coming off one of his best seasons and was voted the American League's most valuable player in 1936.

"Lou Gehrig is seriously thinking of plunging into the moves to handle a Tarzan role," wrote Edward T. Murphy in the New York Sun on October 21, 1936. "If they make a monkey out of Lou in Hollywood, the pitchers who couldn't do it in the American League last season will clamor for the recipe. Gehrig will go for the Tarzan stuff in a big way provided it doesn't call for getting paid off in peanuts and leopard skins."

Gehrig even went so far as to pose for photographers in a lion skin, and perform the famous Tarzan yell. But author Burroughs wasn't impressed with the Yankees slugger. Just prior to Lesser selecting Morris for the role, Burroughs sent the following letter to Gehrig: "I have seen several pictures of you as Tarzan and paid about $50 for newspaper clippings on the subject. I want to congratulate you on being a swell first baseman."

On April 8, 1937, Lesser held a press conference in Hollywood to announce that

Glenn Morris would become the screen's latest Tarzan. In a report by the Associated Press, Lesser said, "We signed Morris for one thing, because we wanted an audience to know it was really Tarzan leaping from tree to tree and hurdling barriers, and not a stunt man. Who would do it better than a world champion?"

Buried near the end of the article was an interesting comment from Glenn. When asked by a reporter how he would like playing opposite "movie queens," he took the opportunity to say something nice about his new bride: "Shucks, I think my wife is prettier than any of them," he responded.

With the selection process over and the new Tarzan signed and delivered, Lesser said he planned to make five movies with Morris in the lead. Lesser also announced he was looking for a sponsor for a radio weekly Tarzan show, which would also star Morris. Naturally, the focus then turned to pay, and there was a wide disparity in the amounts being talked about.

"When Twentieth Century-Fox decided to make Tarzan pictures, Glenn Morris was given a test and signed for the title role in the jungle series on a two-year contract which will pay him the sum of $250,000," reported PIC Magazine. The San Francisco Call-Bulletin paper ran an article on April 9 saying that Morris had signed to do five films for a total of $500,000.

But the amount of money he was being paid apparently was a part of the Hollywood hype. While the report of a possible $500,000 was very impressive, the real amount was probably closer to $10,000 a film. Decades later, his sister, Virginia Baxter, said that Glenn never received anywhere near the amounts reported in the papers. She added that his disenchantment over his Tarzan salary eventually soured him on the movie world and hastened his decline in life.

Arriving in Hollywood amid considerable publicity, Morris was very enthused about his prospects for a film career. Pete Smith, who specialized in making movie shorts, signed Glenn up for a ten-minute film for MGM entitled "Decathlon Champion." It revolved around Glenn's decathlon training and eventual triumph in Berlin. The film offered clips of Glenn supposedly back home in Simla, and even included scenes of him jumping over a cow as it stood passively chewing grass down by a stream. There are also clips of him in training in college, with Coach Hughes timing him in various events.

Acting also as the film's narrator, Pete Smith understood what it was that made Morris such a great athlete, and informed the audience:

"Here was a guy who didn't worry so much about form as he did about results. A kid with a great ambition, not always the personification of poetry in motion, but a lad who grasped fundamentals quickly and applied his fine natural physical coordination and power. The answer was found in his scoresheet. Mastering the javelin throw, Glenn Morris polished off a campaign of patience, study and hard work."

The documentary was well done and made to look like it was shot in Simla, but actually it was filmed in the foothills around Hollywood, and at an area college.

Shortly after completing the documentary, Glenn met with Burroughs and Lesser for a series of publicity shots. The newspapers were full of short stories about the latest film Tarzan, and his photo appeared everywhere. But before shooting began on

Tarzan, he was booked for a small but important role in a comedy, "Hold that Co-Ed," also being produced by Twentieth Century-Fox. It seemed as though the entire world was opening up to him and all he had to do was sign a few papers and display his considerable athletic abilities.

"He was excited, my lord; he even had the folks come down to California," said Jack. "Dad was working in a little town just south of Seattle. In California, Glenn helped dad get a caretaker's job for some of the stars. He pruned trees and tended the orchards for Al Jolson and Ruby Keeler. Dad thought that was great. He loved it." Glenn even talked Jack into coming to California.

"He wrote me a letter insisting I come on out. 'Get out of those mines, I got a job for you,' he said. But I never did quite get along in Hollywood. I never found much of a job, and Glenn didn't have the pull he thought he did."

"Hold That Co-Ed" was a pleasant effort that featured such Hollywood notables as John Barrymore, George Murphy, Joan Davis and Jack Haley. Morris is the fifteenth name on the cast list at movie's end.

Barrymore was already a Hollywood legend, while Murphy was a more than adequate leading man who went on to become a two-term United States Senator from California; Haley gained considerable fame a year later by playing the Tin Man in the "The Wizard of Oz." Davis was a comedienne in the Lucille Ball mold who even had her own television show, entitled "I Married Joan," many years later.

"Hold That Co-Ed" rated three stars out of a possible four by TV Guide in its April 20, 1991, edition. "The campaign of a scoundrelly governor (John Barrymore) hits a snag because of a college football team," reads the capsule summary.

Glenn appears early in the film wearing a white letter sweater, with a big S on it (for the mythical State University, not Simla). He is seen throughout, often next to Murphy, who plays the head football coach. With his slicked-back, dark hair and angular good looks, Morris stands out in many scenes. He also has several opportunities to display glimpses of his athletic prowess. As Spencer, a running back and defensive back on the State team, he intercepts a pass in one scene and returns it for a long touchdown. Wearing jersey number 22, he is also evident in many other plays, and holds the ball for Davis each time she comes in to kick the extra point.

Spencer is State's captain for the big battle with archrival Clayton at the film's conclusion. Injured near the end of the game, Spencer watches from the sidelines, along with Murphy and a wild-eyed, wild-haired Barrymore, as Davis scores the winning touchdown in a very amusing scene. Battling hurricane-like winds, Davis staggers toward the goal line in slow motion, with the Clayton tacklers close behind. The winds are so severe that the players are unable to make any headway....until at last Davis flops face down into the end zone for the winning touchdown, just as the wind blows the goal posts over.

"Hold That Co-Ed" is decades ahead of its time by allowing a female, and not a muscular male, to score the crucial points. Morris does a solid job in all his scenes, including a dance routine where Murphy leads the football team down the street to the governor's mansion. The world's greatest athlete is clearly evident in the second row, dancing and singing along with all the other extras.

TOP and BOTTOM: Glenn was the subject of a short film made by Pete Smith called "Decathlon Champion".

LEFT: Glenn and Charlotte take some time off to go swimming at a Los Angeles club.

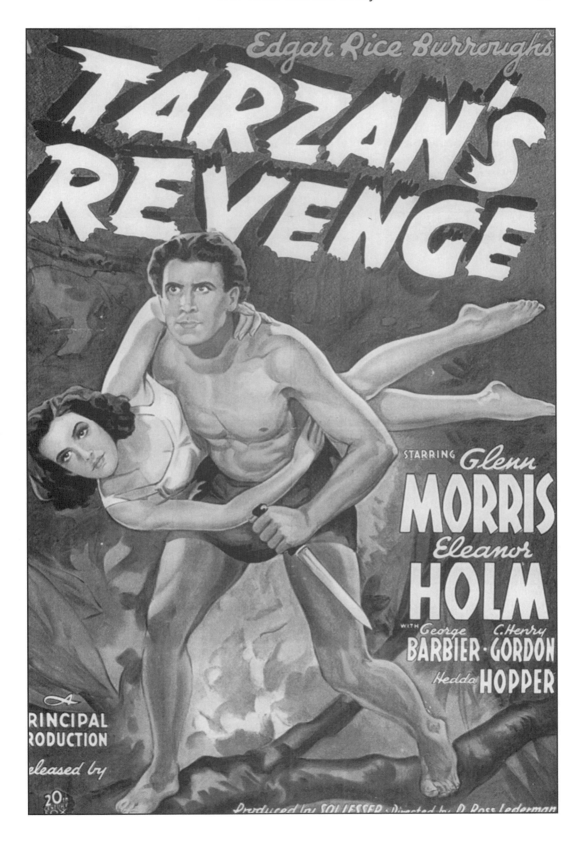

RIGHT: Glenn (center) confronts new head football coach George Murphy (left) in a scene from "Hold That Co-Ed." Glenn appeared in the movie while waiting for filming to begin on Tarzan.

TOP: Glenn and his friends attempt to toss Murphy in a well.

RIGHT: The "S" on the lettersweater Glenn is wearing stands for "State," not Simla.

RIGHT: "Hold That Co-Ed' was a cute college football movie that gave Glenn his first shot at acting.

TOP: As the star running back Spencer, Glenn (in helmet, behind coach) listens as the football coach (played by George Murphy) discusses a point with a co-ed (played by Joan Davis). Murphy later became a U.S. Senator.

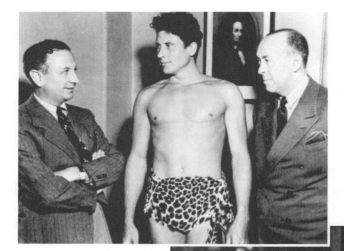

LEFT: Glenn meets with Tarzan author Edgar Rice Burroughs (right) and Sol Lesser, the producer of "Tarzan's Revenge."

TOP: Outside the studio office, Glenn warms up prior to a hard day's work in the jungle.

LEFT: Playing football was a great way for Tarzan to relax between scenes on the set in Los Angeles.

(Tarzan photos courtesy of Edgar Rice Burroughs, Inc.)

In one of his
best photos
as Tarzan,
Glenn Morris
poses with
a jungle friend.
Notice the
footwear Glenn
is wearing to
protect his feet
against
the hazards
of playing
the Apeman.

Though they
were on the
same Olympic
team in 1936,
Glenn and
Eleanor Holm
had no real or
reel chemistry
when in
Hollywood,
and were not
friends on or
off the set.

In the most exciting and action-packed scene in the movie, Tarzan struggles with the natives on a rope bridge high above a river. After chasing the natives away, Tarzan dives from the bridge into the river.

**RIGHT:
One of the
bad guys gets
a stern look
from Tarzan
during this
scene from
"Tarzan's
Revenge."**

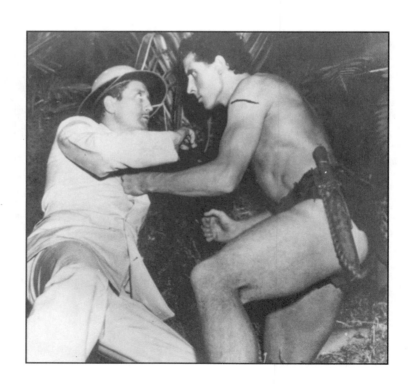

LEFT: Eleanor does not look at all pleased with the way things are going in this scene from the movie.

BELOW: The happy jungle couple.

BELOW: In a Hollywood publicity photo, Glenn goes cheek to cheek with an unidentified actress.

Tarzan and his pals

Animals play a key role in all Tarzan movies, and that was certainly the case with Glenn in "Tarzan's Revenge."

Tarzan and Cheetah do the "jungle jitterbug"

A key element of any movie is the pre-release publicity work. Glenn was featured in photos showcasing his great athletic skills (left) and with Eleanor Holm, in a variety of poses.... including one rather strange shot (below).

The script called for Tarzan to carry Eleanor around in some less than
glamorous positions. In the top photo, Hedda Hopper (in white shirt)
expresses some concern over the way her daughter is being handled.
Hopper left acting to become one of Hollywood's top gossip columnists.

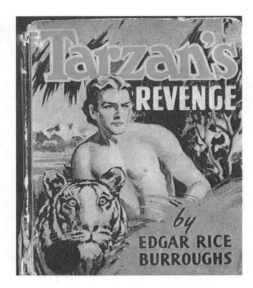

Memorabilia from Glenn's Tarzan movie can bring a good price
from collectors. The Big Little Book (left) was published
in 1938, as was the title lobby card (below).
The video of the movie (top right) is available on
the internet on a regular basis.

Although four Olympians and a professional football player all held the role at one time, certainly the best all-around athlete ever to play Tarzan was Glenn Morris. In this photo, Glenn shows that he also had the physical appearance to be a great movie Tarzan. By nearly all accounts, a weak script and poor production values were the main problem with "Tarzan's Revenge," not the efforts of Glenn Morris.

Glenn Morris

Glenn and Charlotte visited Edgar Rice Burroughs in Hawaii on New Year's Eve of 1937, shortly before "Tarzan's Revenge" was released, on January 7, 1938. It was a happy occasion for all three....but the joy was not to last for long. Shortly after, Glenn and Charlotte divorced and Burroughs could not have been pleased with the way the movie wound up, being panned by all critics.

(Photo courtesy of Lee Chase)

In a studio pose for publicity, Glenn shows once again that he had the physical appearance to be an ideal movie Tarzan.
(Photo courtesy of Ralph Brown)

Ironically, Murphy's father, Mike Murphy, was a legendary track coach at Yale and the University of Pennsylvania for nearly twenty-six years, and served as head track coach of the United States Olympic team in 1912. That was the year Jim Thorpe electrified the world by winning both the pentathlon and decathlon in Stockholm. It's not hard to imagine that George Murphy knew about Glenn's great accomplishments in Berlin, and sought him out for some athletic conversation between scenes.

In retrospect, decades later, it seems the film could have provided a springboard to similar roles for Morris. It's not at all unreasonable to assume he could have established himself as a competent character actor, learning his trade and moving up the ladder slowly, in the same fashion as Herman Brix was doing, and as Audie Murphy did after World War II.

But, it wasn't to be. Of the four Olympic heroes to play Tarzan, Morris was the least successful in building a film career. Most of the blame has to be placed on the poor showing his Tarzan film made at the box office. The fact of the matter is that his Tarzan movie was ill-conceived from the very start.

Lesser had signed another Olympic champion to be the female lead — Eleanor Holm. Despite being booted off the Olympic team just two years earlier, Holm was a very big name nationally, due to both her athletic exploits and the Olympic flap. During her career, she set a total of seven world records and she held twenty-nine national titles of one sort or another. Before winning her gold medal in 1932, she had even been on the 1928 Olympic team at the age of fourteen!

Still smarting over what she perceived as a huge injustice in 1936, she was flirting with a career in film. Most of all, though, she was looking for a good time. And Hollywood seemed like an ideal place to find it....even if it did mean she would be reunited with Glenn.

"It was all such a mess. I had been around; I was no baby," she said of the 1936 flap. "Hell, I married Art Jarrett after the '32 Games. He was the star at the Coconut Grove, and I went to work singing for his band. I used to take a mike and get up in front of the band in a white bathing suit and a white cowboy hat and high heels. I'd sing 'I'm an Old Cowhand.' I wasn't much of a singer, but I was okay with a mike." *(24)*

Screenwriters Robert Lee Johnson and Jay Vann produced a very weak script, one in which Tarzan saves Holm from being forced to join a sultan's large harem. Holm was called Eleanor throughout the film — "being so well known, Eleanor would not have been acceptable to the general public as Jane," said Lesser — causing confusion if not outright embarrassment at the end of the movie when Tarzan and Eleanor are apparently headed for a jungle relationship.

In addition, the musical score was terrible. The movie, entitled "Tarzan's Revenge," was filmed on the back lots at Twentieth Century-Fox. It began with Tarzan rescuing Holm from what looks to be little more than a mudhole, and ends with Morris carrying Holm away from a harem, the petite swimmer tucked under one arm.

Years later, it was rumored that Morris and Holm did not particularly care for one another, and their interaction on screen would hardly dispute that rumor. They were both wooden and uncomfortable. The weak plot did nothing to help the star.

"As actors we were both so bad," Holm said in 1991. "I was terrible. And he was worse than I was. The movie was just horrible. I thought I was awful. I was a lousy actress. Period."

Holm knew that Morris was one of the athletes who felt she should have been dismissed from the Olympic team, and signed a petition to that affect. Naturally, that opinion didn't set well at the time with Holm, and made for an uncomfortable relationship when they found themselves together on a movie set less than two years later. However, by 2001, she had made peace with the situation.

"I didn't dislike Glenn Morris, really," she said in a phone interview from her home in Miami. "We just came from such different backgrounds. There wasn't any chemistry between us, we had nothing in common. I knew that he had signed the petition, but we never talked about it on the set. I don't know if he knew that I knew that.

"I think his main problem was that he took himself so seriously. I was just there to have some fun; I knew I wasn't an actress. He complained about everything, actually. Every hair had to be in place, and he was always questioning the film crew about things he didn't know anything about. Many of them resented it."

But Glenn was only reverting to a process that had worked extremely well for him in his athletic endeavors. He had become the world's best all-around athlete by studying all facets of the decathlon, and paying tremendous attention to detail, then working with great devotion and determination. It was a key element of his success formula. It was only natural that he would bring the same type of devotion and intensity to his next project, which was film.

Holm paused, reflecting back on the movie set of six decades previous.

"It's not that Glenn was a bad guy. He was sort of....well, he just didn't know any better. He just wanted to get ahead in life."

The two stars certainly had little chemistry on the set, and they never saw each other again after the film was finished. In fact, she knew nothing of what happened to Glenn during the war years or at the end of his life.

The film debuted on January 7, 1938, and was widely panned by critics. While the movie is nearly seventy minutes long, Tarzan only is on screen for about ten minutes. Furthermore, Morris only says four words the entire film! He utters "Tarzan" twice, "Eleanor" once....and mutters "Good!" while eating grapes.

"Even the youngsters, at which this type of production is aimed, will not be much impressed," said Variety.

"Its greatest lack is in the two leads," wrote John Mosher, of New York magazine. " (Both) have many rows to hoe before they can be called actors, either good or bad." Among the other actors was Hedda Hopper, who played Eleanor's mother and then went on to a long career as a top Hollywood gossip writer.

Another magazine, Liberty, called Holm "one of the year's worst actresses."

In his action scenes, Morris came off as lithe and agile. He moved well, and looked the part of a man who had been raised in an extremely physical environment. He "certainly had the physical attributes to play Tarzan," said author David Fury in his book, *Kings of the Jungle*. But the lack of dialogue — he has just four words in the entire film — forced him to rely almost exclusively on body language and facial expressions, skills for which he had little training." *(25)*

The movie didn't even play well with some of Glenn's relatives in Missouri.

Agnes Morris Stratton, his aunt, went to the movie at the insistence of her son, Eldon. When pressed for her impression of the film, she had little good to say.

"They had him swinging through the trees with few clothes on and he couldn't talk, only grunt and gesture and make some sounds," said Agnes.

"Agnes thought they had portrayed her honored nephew in a very degrading (manner)," wrote Jean Bird in her family history. "She didn't really appreciate it at all. She was let down by the whole movie."

While the film drew poor reviews even among his closest relatives, Morris also had to suffer a rather uncomfortable moment at a Hollywood party, where he was introduced as the new Tarzan. Lupe Velez, an actress who was aptly nicknamed the Mexican Spitfire, was married to Weissmuller at the time "Tarzan's Revenge" was in production. When she heard Morris proclaimed the new Tarzan at the party, Velez walked up to him, kicked him in the shin, and shouted, "You are not heem! There is only one Tarzan, and that's my Johneee!" *(26)*

After her role in "Tarzan's Revenge," Holm teamed with Weissmuller for a summer of shows at the New York World's Fair of 1939. Billy Rose, a master showman, signed the pair to perform in his aquatic spectacle. It was a huge success, and Weissmuller and Holm seemed to get along very well, according to reports. Holm also got along well with Billy Rose. She divorced Art Jarrett and married Rose, who dumped Fanny Brice (the legendary "Funny Girl") to wed Eleanor.

The problems in Glenn's life weren't limited to the Tarzan set and reaction to the film. Just a year after arriving in Hollywood full of high hopes and great expectations, Glenn and Charlotte were experiencing severe marital problems. The post-Olympic Glenn Morris seemed to be far different from the man she had met in college and had fallen in love with. Somehow, the hugely contrasting Olympic experience and the Hollywood "rush" had exerted a negative pull on him. Or was it a suppressed love for Leni Riefenstahl, a romantic feeling so strong that Glenn was unable to cope with it while married to another woman?

"There were lots of things going wrong at that time," said Caroline Tucker, Charlotte's sister. "He was playing polo in California with people like Will Rogers and cavorting around town, coming home late. I think he was trying hard to be someone in Hollywood, but felt out of place. He came from a very poor background of bean farmers, and he seemed to always be trying to overcome his poverty."

Caroline said she had seen evidence of insecurity and an obsessive drive back in their college days. She was just one class behind Charlotte at Colorado A&M, and her husband, Omar Tucker, had been an athlete at the college who also knew Glenn. Looking back over five decades, she didn't feel that her sister and Glenn were a good match.

"Char wasn't very gregarious or outgoing," said Caroline, "and Glenn was very quiet. He wouldn't look at you directly when talking to him. He was big man on campus because of his great athletic prowess, but he didn't really have a good personality. He seemed to have a chip on his shoulder; maybe it was from his poor background.

"Omar knew him from athletics, but didn't feel at all close to him, either. I don't think very many people did."

Former Colorado A&M football player Norman Cable, who Glenn had mentored while serving as a graduate assistant coach, remembered Charlotte as "beautiful and charming" and said he "greatly admired her." He also recalled the last time he saw Glenn was in the fall of 1938, in Los Angeles.

"My professional football team, the Cincinnati Bengals, was playing in Los Angeles," he wrote. "During the short intermission at the half, I was told a gentleman was standing by to see me. He had persisted, indicating he was an old friend, and was allowed to enter our dressing room. Here was my old friend and punting instructor….we had a brief but very emotional visit. That was the last time I saw Glenn."

With Morris caught up in his determination to make his mark in Hollywood and struggling to do so, Charlotte grew disillusioned and returned to Sterling. After a brief effort at reconciliation, she filed for divorce. She found a job in a Denver department store, and did some modeling work on the side. She remarried, and moved back to California with her new husband, and began a teaching career in Los Angeles. They had two children, but eventually divorced. Charlotte returned to Fort Collins in the late 1970s, married a third time, and died there of cancer in 1979. After she left Glenn Morris in 1938, she never saw him again.

Their separation marked another huge turning point in Glenn's life. Charlotte had been his confidant and training partner during the happy years in Fort Collins, as they shared the dream of an Olympic gold medal. They had been a tremendous team, working toward a united goal. But Berlin's triumphs, and perhaps Leni Riefenstahl, had doomed the relationship. All of the good fortune that had come his way up to this point was about to turn sour. The glory ride was nearly over for Glenn Morris, and his nation was about to be catapulted into a horrific world war by the same man who had once idolized the Colorado athlete.

The Real Jungle

In Hollywood, Johnny Weissmuller had outlasted his other Olympic challengers as the "reel" Tarzan. But while Weissmuller was reaping the benefits of being King of the Jungle, midway to making his record twelve Tarzan films, Glenn Morris found himself immersed in a real-life drama that was destined to drastically alter the course of his life. Along with most Americans, Morris became deeply embroiled in World War II, the only one of the four Olympic Tarzans to ever fight for his country in the armed services.

After "Tarzan's Revenge" received such poor reviews and his marriage ended, Glenn was struggling to earn a living. The funds from "Tarzan's Revenge" and "Hold That Co-Ed" quickly evaporated, and he needed to have a steady income. The $250,000 contract, if it ever existed, was contingent upon him being placed in continuous roles, and none were being offered. With no movies on the horizon, he played a little semi-professional football for a team called the Hollywood Bears, and then returned to Colorado. He worked as an insurance agent in Denver for two years, and in 1940 landed a tryout with the Detroit Lions of the National Football League. The Lions had drafted Morris back in 1934 after his final year of college football, but he had passed up the opportunity to concentrate on the decathlon instead. The team had tried to sign him again after the Olympics, but he had chosen the movie world. Now, six years after graduation from college, he was ready to give professional football a try.

He endured a rigorous training camp, and on opening day was a member of the Lions' starting lineup, at right end. He took the field on September 15 against the St. Louis Cardinals. The game ended in a 0-0 tie....but not before Morris suffered a broken leg. His NFL career was over in less time than it took to sit through "Tarzan's Revenge." It was another crushing setback for the kid from Simla.

The star of the Detroit Lions that year was another Colorado athlete, Byron "Whizzer" White. While Morris had been preparing for the Olympics in Fort Collins, White was tearing up the gridiron down the road in Boulder, at the University of Colorado. He was a first team All-American halfback in 1937, and signed with the NFL's Pittsburgh team in 1938 for $15,800 – at that time the largest contract in the history of professional football!

In 1939, White took a year off to study as a Rhodes Scholar, and was subsequently traded to Detroit prior to the 1940 season. He led the entire league in rushing that season with 514 yards, and then retired in 1941 to pursue a law career. President John F. Kennedy named White to the U.S. Supreme Court in 1962, and he served in that capacity for thirty-one years, retiring in 1993.

In 1988, Justice White answered a letter inquiring about his recollections of Glenn Morris. His words were brief, but still provide a glimpse into Morris's life at the time.

"Although I, of course, knew of Glenn Morris and his athletic performances before 1940, I did not meet him personally until then," wrote the Supreme Court Justice. "I found him an agreeable but a seemingly shy man, one who wanted to do his very best, but not sure of his own future."

If Glenn seemed unsure of his future prior to the injury, one can only imagine how he must have felt after suffering the devastating setback. He undoubtedly left Detroit with a growing sense of disillusionment. All of his life he had used his tremendous work ethic and fierce determination to succeed. Those two characteristics had carried him to stirring successes at Colorado State College and the Olympic Games, and had even opened the door to the glamorous movie world. But somehow his fortunes had changed dramatically in the last three years. Hollywood had not worked out to his satisfaction, his marriage had fallen apart in less than two years, and his dreams of playing in the National Football League were shattered. But the worst was still to come!

Morris returned to Denver in the late fall of 1940 and resumed his insurance career. He was beginning to settle into the monotony of day-to-day existence. His prospects were drab compared to all he had been through; fading fast were the huge dreams of the past ten years – replaced by a gnawing sense of the ordinary. Perhaps he spent most of his evenings dreaming of Berlin….the overwhelming thrill of victory, of his golden moment on the awards stand, the national anthem of the United States playing loudly, and of bending down to allow Eva Braun to place the laurel wreath on his head. But most certainly, he had thoughts of Leni Riefenstahl. According to his brother Jack, memories of Leni and what "could have been" were with him all the rest of his life.

Like most Americans, he undoubtedly followed the news of Nazi Germany with considerable interest and trepidation. As Hitler began to make his plans of conquest known to the world, most people recoiled in shock. For the members of the 1936 Olympic team – men like Jesse Owens and Glenn Morris – the activities of the Third Reich constituted a much more personal experience. They held a perspective that few other Americans could imagine….they had actually shared the same time and space with Hitler and his henchmen. While millions of Americans were growing to despise the very name of Hitler, Glenn Morris had to come to terms with the fact that Hitler had cheered him on to victory….had actually sat in the stands and had applauded his efforts wildly!

The case can be made that the Berlin Olympics helped falsely convince Hitler that Germans really were a master race, and should be the rulers of the world. Germany had won the medal showdown by a 181-124 margin over second place America. The Germans earned a total of thirty-three gold medals to just twenty-four by the Americans. And the many victories made Hitler and his leaders flush with excitement over the plans they had been developing.

"The illusions offered to the Germans and to the world by the results of the 1936

Olympics were emboldening to the aggressors and were debilitating to the scheduled victims in that war," wrote Mandell. "The confident loosing of the ambitions of the new Germans was the worst consequence of the onerous symbolic burdens that the Olympic Games and their athletic participants had taken on since the Games were revived in 1896." (27)

Hitler's troops invaded Austria in March of 1938, and took control of Czechoslovakia a year later. On September 1, 1939, Germany moved against Poland, sending troops marching into the country. Two days later, Great Britain and France declared war on Germany. There was no turning back. In rapid succession, Hitler took over Denmark, Norway, the Netherlands, Belgium, Luxembourg and France.

Trying to maintain an isolationist policy, America watched nervously from across the Atlantic as Italy joined Germany, and France surrendered. But on the morning of December 7, 1941, the Japanese bombing attack of Pearl Harbor thrust the United States into the war full throttle. Some 180 Japanese bombers and torpedo planes unleashed their sneak attack several minutes before 8 a.m.; the American casualties were shocking. Nearly 250 U.S. aircraft, four battleships, three destroyers and three cruisers were destroyed. An estimated 3,581 American servicemen were killed or wounded. Fortunately, the largest part of the carrier fleet was at sea at the time of the attack and was thereby spared.

At the moment the first Japanese bomb was released, there was no longer any option left for the United States; a sleeping giant had indeed been awakened.

Morris entered the United States Navy on October 5, 1942, as an enlisted man, and took two months of basic training in Norfolk, Virginia. He spent six months at the Naval Training Center in San Diego, and then six more months with a training unit in Seattle. He applied for officer's status and attended officers' school in San Diego. He was commissioned as a lieutenant junior grade (JG) on May 11, 1944, and was assigned to Beach Battalion D, in Oceanside, California. In October of 1944, Morris was assigned to the USS Banner (APA60), an attack transport named for Banner County in western Nebraska. The ship was commissioned on September 16, 1944, and reported to San Francisco for its first mission, the transporting of troops to Milne Bay and Hollandia in New Guinea. Morris was to join the Banner in New Guinea.

With a length of eighteen hundred miles and a width of four hundred miles, New Guinea is the world's second largest island, behind only Greenland. A tropical wilderness situated close to the northernmost tip of Australia, it was the site of bitter fighting between combined Australian and American forces against the Japanese. The Japanese took the island early on in the war, and it was considered a critical jumping off spot for whichever military force controlled it. The Allies took control in July of 1943, and by 1944 it was being used by the Allies as a send-off port for still-contested Pacific islands to the north.

The small islands of the central Pacific were being used by the Japanese forces to form a vast protective ring around the island empire. A poster produced by the National Archives told the story: "If the Americans were going to defeat the Japanese, they would have to penetrate the ring by capturing these islands. Once in Allied hands, these tiny dots on the map would become bases for operations ever closer to the

Japanese home islands. They would provide landing fields from which bombers could attack Japanese cities. Thus, the protective ring would be transformed into a slowly tightening noose around Japan.

"Taking these strategic islands made for some of the bloodiest fighting of the war. Japanese fought to the death rather than surrender." *(28)*

The USS Banner, with Lieutenant Commander J.R. Pace in command, arrived at Milne Bay in New Guinea on November 17, ready to take on new crewmembers. Among the latter was a naval officer from dirt-poor Simla, Colorado. And he made quite an impression.

"I'll never forget the first time I saw Glenn Morris," said Jim Larson of Denver, Colorado. "He came aboard the Banner in New Guinea. I was captain of the softball team for the enlisted men, and we were playing the officers' team when I first saw him. He came striding out to the field and watched the game. He wanted to be on the enlisted men's team. Morris was a lieutenant, but he didn't want to play with the officers, and he told them so."

Morris was the sort of man who made a lasting impression on anyone who came in contact with him, according to Larson.

"He had arms as big as legs, and a huge chest. I was only eighteen at the time, but he was very impressive to look at. He had a passion for the enlisted men, and they knew that and respected him for that. He had a mind of his own, that's for sure. Can you imagine being with a group of officers, and telling them you wanted to play on the enlisted men's team instead? But they didn't say anything. Boy, were they scared of him."

Larson returned to Colorado and began a teaching career after the war. He served as a principal in a Denver grade school for many years. By 2001, he was long retired but enjoyed reflecting back on the short time he spent with Glenn Morris.

"Once, the captain (Pace) of the ship was standing on the deck talking to us, and Lt. Morris was right behind him. He was mimicking the captain, making faces, over and over. I think the captain knew it, but he never turned around or said a word to him. He was scared of Morris. He just had that air about him."

Larson had a run-in with Lt. Commander Pace that directly involved Morris. Larson was asked to pick up the ship's mail, and was dressed casually. It was over 118 degrees, and he was not on official duty at the time. But as Larson approached the ship, Pace was watching him, and had Larson brought to his office.

"It was a captain's mast, and the captain (Pace) was going to throw me in the brig, apparently because I wasn't in official attire," explained Larson, still showing emotion nearly four decades after the event. "I was shocked, I couldn't believe it. I hadn't done anything wrong. Lt. Morris got word of what was happening and came into the office. He told the captain, 'I'm the beachmaster and this man is in the beach party. He's under my command and I'm not going to allow you to do this.'

"Even though the captain outranked Morris, the captain backed down. That was the end of it," said Larson.

Though just a teenager and only one year removed from high school at the time, Larson was able to establish a slight rapport with the former Olympian, perhaps because they were both native Coloradans.

"He was a real loner. He invited me into his cabin once, when I was delivering a communiqué," said Larson. "He showed me this photo of a woman, a very attractive blonde, and said she was his girl. You could tell he really hated to leave the States, and she seemed to mean a great deal to him.

"He wasn't close to anyone that I could see. We had been told he was a celebrity, but we didn't know how big an athletic star he really was. He had an air of cockiness about him, but he never talked about being Tarzan, or an Olympic champion. He wasn't arrogant, just cocky, in a confident sort of way."

Larson also remembers the way that Morris looked at someone when he was upset. It was an intimidating stare that made the person he was confronting think twice before challenging him.

"He had gray eyes, and if he looked you straight in the eyes, it made you take notice right away. He wasn't a man to be trifled with, that's for sure. We all knew that."

Larson said he did not learn the extent of Morris's Olympic achievements until a year after Larson left the Banner. He was in the state of Washington on another assignment, and was watching a newsreel at a movie theatre with other Naval personnel.

"All of a sudden, a special (probably the short documentary made by Pete Smith) came on, and it was all about Lt. Morris. It showed him winning the Olympics in Berlin. I was shocked. I turned around to everyone and said, 'Hey, I served under Lt. Morris on the Banner.' They all said, 'Yeah....right, sure you did.' I was really surprised to see the newsreel, and proud to have served with him."

As an officer on the USS Banner, Richard Beidleman held a considerably different opinion of Morris. He was already on the Banner when Morris arrived, and in 2001 still had definite opinions on Morris – not all of them flattering.

"He was an egotist....he carried news clippings of his Olympic days in his wallet and would pull them out and show them to the officers on deck. That's how we even became aware of who he was," said Beidleman, from his home in Pacific Grove, California.

"When he first came aboard, I was over him in rank. But he did some checking out and found out that in reality he outranked me....so for the rest of the time I served under him. I don't blame him for that, it just seemed kind of silly at the time."

A native of Grand Forks, North Dakota, Beidleman graduated from the University of Colorado in Boulder. He was trained in aircraft recognition, and served for a while as gunnery officer aboard the Banner. He was also in charge of securing movies for the men to watch in the evenings.

"After I found out he had made a Tarzan movie, I tried and tried and tried to get it to show the men," said Beidleman with a chuckle. "Oh, how I tried to get that movie. I thought the men would get a real kick out of seeing Lt. Morris swinging through the trees, acting like a jungle man. But I was never able to get it."

Beidleman estimates that he and Morris served together for about a year and says they did not have any serious problems or disagreements. But during that entire time, he does not recall Morris mixing with any of the other officers, or developing a friendship with anyone else on the ship.

"He wasn't anybody you wanted to cozy up to, and we knew it," said Beidleman. "We had a lot of friendships among the officers – we'd go out together on leave. But I don't think he ever went out with us, not once."

Morris had, said Beidleman, "an overpowering and dominating" persona. "He was a huge man. I still have a picture of the officers all standing together, and you can pick him out right away. He was just larger and powerful, and aloof."

Morris had displayed a certain aloofness all through his formative years in Simla, a fact that was not lost on Jean Bird, or on several of the men who knew him well. Though he was elected to class offices in college, it was most likely due to his athletic prowess. Charlotte Edward's sister and husband found him aloof, and so did his Olympic teammates.

His days as a naval officer aboard the USS Banner most likely reinforced his feelings of solitude. Life in the Pacific theatre was a rugged ordeal for the fighting men of World War II. Ernie Pyle, the war's most famous correspondent, saw a tremendous difference between the European theatre and the Pacific theatre.

"The methods of war, the attitude toward it, the homesickness, the distances, the climate – everything is different from what we have known in the European war," Ernie Pyle wrote in a dispatch on February 16, 1945. "Distance is the main thing. I don't mean distance from America so much, for our war in Europe is a long way from home too. I mean distances after you get right on the battlefield.

"For the whole Western Pacific is our battlefield now, and whereas distances in Europe are hundreds of miles at most, out there they are thousands. And there's nothing in between but water."

Great distances were involved in the war with Japan. Manila and San Francisco were separated by nearly 7,000 miles of ocean, with only a few small islands in between. Tokyo was some 5,500 miles from America's west coast. The immense, never-ending body of water could become almost as intimidating as the sight of enemy platoons pouring over a bluff. And there were other factors to weigh heavy on a man's mind.

"There is another enemy out here that we did not know so well in Europe, and that is monotony," wrote Pyle. "Oh sure, war everywhere is monotonous in its dreadfulness. But out here even the niceness of life gets monotonous. The days are warm and on our established island bases the food is good and the mail service is fast and there's little danger from the enemy and the days go by in their endless sameness and they drive you nuts. They sometimes call it going 'pineapple crazy.'"

To a man like Morris – who grew up on a dryland farm in Colorado, surrounded by unending pastures and the majestic Rocky Mountains in the far distance – sailing the Pacific must have been a sobering experience. In fact, the combination of a number of factors working on him, including the vastness of the Pacific, might have been more than Glenn Morris could cope with. He probably felt subtle and deep psychological pressures by the enforced idleness. Such pressures would lie dormant until pushed to the front by the full impact of the combat which he would eventually encounter.

"Our high rate of returning mental cases is discussed frankly in the island and service newspapers," added Pyle. "A man doesn't have to be under fire in the front lines to have more than he can take without breaking."

Such factors may have been at work on Morris's psyche. As a man of intense action, sitting and playing the waiting game was sure to be difficult for him.

In early October of 1944, the American and Japanese flights collided in the Battle of Leyte Gulf, off the Philippines. The Americans emerged victorious, sinking three Japanese battleships, four aircraft carriers and ten cruisers. By October 20, the American forces were in control.

"The battle also marked the first Japanese use of Kamikaze aircraft loaded with explosives and piloted by flyers who committed suicide by ramming U.S. vessels," reported documents from the National Archives. "The Kamikazes damaged the American fleet but did not prevent the landing on Leyte Island."

Two months after the epic battle, on December 30, the USS Banner, with Lt. Glenn Morris aboard, departed from Cape Sansapor, New Guinea.

"The Banner missed Iwo Jima, thank God," said Jim Larson. Born from a volcanic explosion eons ago and only eight square miles in size, Iwo Jima had little to offer the world other than a few sulfur mines and a sugar refinery. Then the Japanese made it the site of an important airbase near the start of the war in the Pacific.

The island was captured by American forces in March of 1945 after terrible battles and horrendous suffering. The cost to U.S. troops was extremely heavy. Of the twenty radiomen who attended radio school with Larson, fifteen of them saw combat on Iwo Jima; only one survived. The desolate rock was immortalized by the John Wayne film "Sands of Iwo Jima," and by the famous photo of U.S. Marines erecting a flag at the summit.

Bypassing Iwo Jima, the Banner headed toward the Philippines, a diverse group of islands which sprawl over hundreds of miles of ocean off the coast of Southeast Asia, in the Malay Archipelago. Also of volcanic origin, many of the islands are handsomely decorated with rich jungle terrain....a paradise Tarzan would have loved. Of the seven thousand islands, only about four hundred are regularly inhabited. Strategically situated between the Land of the Rising Sun and the United States' most western outpost, Hawaii, they were a crucial battleground during the war.

The USS Banner arrived in the Philippines eleven days later, storming into Lingayen Gulf on January 9. But the ship went to the wrong beach, one where severe fighting had already taken place.

"There were bodies all over in the water," Larson recalled, his voice low. "We turned about and headed for White Beach. There, we finally landed and were told to dig in."

As beachmaster, Morris was in charge of getting the men from the USS Banner to solid ground. As the landing craft headed toward the beaches and the horrors of war, one wonders if Morris allowed himself to reflect back on those fabulous days in 1936, when he ran and leaped through the Berlin stadium in such impressive fashion. Was Hitler on his mind? Did he recall with anger the memory of the man who saluted him then, and later became responsible for the most horrific war in the history of mankind?

Was he thinking about Leni Riefenstahl, and the magical moments they had shared less than a decade earlier?

It was at this juncture that Morris and Larson were participants in a scene that left an indelible impression on the latter. Fifty years later, Larson talked about the incident as though it were only a week removed. Larson remembers the troops pouring out of the landing crafts, hitting the beach by the hundreds, prepared to fight the Japanese enemy to the death. And then Morris made an appearance as dramatic as any ever envisioned by a Hollywood screenwriter. Larson recalls it thus:

"Lt. Morris ran up behind me and a couple of others on the beach brandishing a submachine gun, swinging it around and shouting. 'Where's my gas mask? I'm going to shoot whoever took my gas mask!' He was yelling wildly, pointing the submachine gun at all of us," recounted Larson, still affected by the scene as he replayed it in his mind.

"We were really shook up. I yelled, 'Wait a minute, Lt. Morris. We don't have your gas mask. Maybe you left it on the landing craft.' He yelled back that he hadn't, and was going to start shooting us all if the person who took his gas mask didn't give it to him immediately. He kept waving that submachine gun all around.

"I jumped up and said, 'I'll go check on the landing craft.' The craft was still sitting there and I ran out to it. I found the gas mask and ran back to the beach and gave it to Lt. Morris. He was very appreciative and settled down right away."

Larson paused, shaken by the re-telling: "I was lucky, I guess. I don't know what would have happened if the gas mask had not been there."

Larson has never quite come to terms with the incident, not even after the passage of five decades.

"It was so strange, and wild. I could just never understand why he acted that way," he said. "Many years later, I heard that he had been in a training incident with a gas mask, and it leaked and he had some troubles with it. Maybe he just sort of panicked, I don't know. I don't know what the answer is."

The answer to Glenn Morris's bizarre actions on the landing at White Beach undoubtedly dwells in the depths of the wartime experience itself, acted upon by the monotony that Pyle describes mixed with what we now know as post-traumatic stress disorder (PTSD). A man of intense inner drive and determination, Morris was a man of action. The endless days and nights in the ship en route to the battle stations – the monotonous desolation of the Pacific – were forces which were probably acting upon Morris's mental makeup in a very profound way.

"Their lives are really empty lives," wrote Pyle on March 17, 1945, about U.S. sailors in the Pacific. "They have their work, and their movies, and their mail, and that's about all they do have. And nothing to look forward to. They never see anybody but themselves, and that gets mighty old. They sail and sail, and never arrive anywhere...."

In Europe, the fighting had turned dramatically against the Nazis. By the winter of 1944, Germany was in serious trouble on all fronts. Hitler moved into the Berlin Fuhrerbunker on January 16, 1945, and remained there until the end. Eva Braun joined him there in April, as the Russians moved in from the east. She and Hitler were married on April 29, and she committed suicide the next day, with a cyanide capsule. Hitler reportedly shot himself with a pistol in the next several minutes, and their bodies were reportedly burned by the Nazis.

In just nine years since Hitler, Braun and Morris had shared center stage during the electricity of the magnificent Olympic Games in Berlin, so much had happened to their world. They had all seen unspeakable horrors and had been immersed in the worst war mankind had ever known. Now, two of them were dead and the third was in the midst of a downhill slide that would result in a premature death. When their lives came to an abrupt end in the bunker beneath Berlin, Eva was thirty-three years of age and Hitler was fifty-six. Glenn Morris, fighting in the South Pacific, was two months shy of his thirty-third birthday.

Like millions of others, in conflicts from the Trojan War to Vietnam, Morris was changed forever by his war experience. His life would never be the same.

In late 1944, Glenn sent two photos to his brother, Jack. They show the former Olympic champion loaded down with canteens and ammunition, dressed in battle fatigues and sporting a submachine gun. He peers out from beneath the thick helmet. On the back of one photo, he wrote: "Easter Day prior to going ashore at Okinawa. I jettison the spare gear as I reach the water. Carry 300 rounds of 45 caliber for the chopper."

In the second photo, Morris wears an expression of grim determination, mouth clenched tight. On the back, he wrote: "Zero hour, D Day at Okinawa. 300 rounds for the chopper. Really loaded. More effective than pine cones at Whitehorse, Calif, remember?"

Beidleman has strong recollections of serving on the USS Banner in late March of 1945, during and after the trip to Okinawa.

"We landed at Okinawa and sent troops into Naha," he said. "We were right next to the Nevada battleship, and it was firing long-range shells over us, night and day, almost non-stop. I would go out on the deck and with binoculars watch our troops on the beach, struggling to go inland. As a beachmaster, Morris was there with them. He went inland to some degree. It was like being in a movie for me, watching from the deck.

"There was lots of fighting. The Japanese were hiding there, and fighting hard. When the men returned from the beach, they brought with them souvenirs from the little graves, or sepulchers. It was like their booty."

The experience would change anybody. And it certainly had a tremendous impact on Glenn Morris, both physically and psychologically.

"He told me about his experiences of going into battle," said his sister, Virginia Baxter, in 2001. "He had to see all those young men hit the beaches, in such terrible circumstances. He said he almost had to pry their hands off of the rails because they were frozen by fear, but that he had to do it. He even dreamed about it."

In 1988, some 45 years after the fact, his younger brother, Wayne, talked about the physical changes he saw in Glenn.

"I was amazed when he came out of the service," said Wayne. "His hair was almost black when he went in. But when he came out, it had turned gray. I was truly amazed when I saw it. He even seemed to walk different, more slumped over. And he had begun smoking, something he had never done before."

Wayne was twelve years younger than Glenn and was just six years old when Glenn went off to college. They did not have the opportunity to interact as much as do brothers who are of a closer age. But Wayne remembered Glenn as "high strung" and felt serving in the Navy was a difficult adjustment for him. "He gave a lot of thought to every decision he made," said Wayne. "And he didn't take changes too well. Being in the service often means you have to do it someone else's way rather than your own, and I think Glenn had trouble adjusting his thinking to that."

Jack also served in the Pacific during World War II. He recalled meeting Glenn shortly after the White Beach incident.

"I was with the Seabees in Okinawa," said Jack in 1989. "I met Glenn there, on Okinawa, when the Banner came in. He was the officer of the day, and I was piped aboard. We talked quite a bit. It was a great day."

But Jack doesn't think Glenn had many great days after White Beach.

"He was a beach master, in charge of landing troops, directing crews this way and that. There were bombs going off everywhere around him. I think he was shell-shocked. For a few of the boys over there, there was so much noise they couldn't deal with it. The Japanese were sending up those little mortars and they were exploding everywhere. Your mind goes kind of goofy in those times."

Then Jack Morris offered a sobering assessment. It was based on the brother he had known while growing up as opposed to the brother who came back from World War II.

"I just don't think Glenn ever quite recovered to the point where he could be his old self again. It's like those boys who came home from Vietnam, and were struggling to fit in again, and be what they were. Glenn could never quite get a hold of himself after that."

The Glenn Morris of Simla, Fort Collins and Berlin had been full of optimism and enthusiasm, eager to face any challenges. But that man had disappeared....and was replaced by a Glenn Morris forged by the bitter disappointments of romance and of Hollywood, and the horrors of war, witnessed and experienced first-hand. The new Glenn Morris was waging a fierce battle deep inside him to hold onto the values he had learned while growing up, but had seen those values blown to bits in a horrible war.

"That would certainly explain his wild behavior on the beach that day," said Larson. "He was beside himself, like he had gone crazy. He kept shouting about his gas mask. Maybe it was because he had already suffered some (psychological) damage."

In his powerful book, *Achilles in Vietnam: Combat Trauma and the Undoing of Character*, author Jonathon Shay describes such action as being in the "berserker" state. He explains the person is virtually out of his mind when in that mental state.

"The berserker is figuratively – sometimes literally – blind to everything but his destructive aim. He cannot see the distinction between civilian and combatant or even the distinction between comrade or enemy." That seems to explain the situation Glenn

Morris was in on the beach that particular day.

The war took a severe toll on thousands of men and women, on both sides of the Pacific. It didn't distinguish between the average fellow and the star. Nile Kinnick, young Heisman Trophy winner (1939) from the University of Iowa, was killed at the age of twenty-four in 1943 when his plane went into the Gulf of Paria on an exercise run; the Sullivan Brothers from Waterloo, Iowa....all five of them....perished when their ship was torpedoed in a savage sea battle at the crack of dawn on November 13, 1942, in the battle of Guadalcanal, in the South Pacific. A young Navy officer named John F. Kennedy almost lost his life in August of 1943 when his PT boat was sunk by Japanese in the South Pacific, off the Solomon Islands.

Audie Murphy of Texas survived the traumas of World War II, having fought all over Europe while still less than twenty years of age. He became the war's most decorated soldier, and returned home to a hero's welcome. He became a Hollywood movie star, and made dozens of films. But his post-war life was a jumbled mess of terrifying memories and suppressed guilt for surviving the war while so many friends had perished. He suffered from post-traumatic stress disorder and was on edge the rest of his life.

"After the war, he never again lived in his home county or state. And nobody who knew him felt that he ever became fully adjusted," wrote Don Graham in his Murphy biography, *No Name on the Bullet. (30)*

Like Murphy, Glenn Morris never returned to his home county or state to live. And he also never became fully adjusted.

Vernon Morris, a cousin of Glenn's, was asked what memories he harbors of Glenn. There aren't many, but those he does have also point to a man who had begun to withdraw from normal social functions.

"I didn't really know Glenn — I wish I would have gotten to know him better," said Vernon, still living on a farm near Simla in 2001. "I used to see him at family gatherings when I was quite small. I was only sixteen when he won the Olympics. I would see Jack at family gatherings after World War II, but never Glenn. I attended all of them, but Glenn never came back. Not once."

The state of Colorado, like all other states, paid a heavy price for the war. A total of 138,832 men enlisted....one out of every eight residents in the state! Approximately 2,700 died as a result of their service. But there were many, many more casualties, some in nerve damage and mental breakdowns:

"...victory exacted a heavy toll. The cost in blood, in nerves, and in the lives of brave young men was a sobering and terrible price," said the book *Colorado and Its People.* (31)

Morris spent four years and eight months in the Navy. He had entered as an enlisted man on October 5, 1942. He served as an officer from May 11, 1944, until discharged on July 1, 1947. The place of separation was Oakland, California. He had served with distinction, and was awarded the Asiatic-Pacific Campaign Medal, two Bronze Service Stars, the American Theater Campaign Medal, the World War II Victory Medal, and the Philippine Liberation Ribbon, with a Bronze Service Star. He also received a letter of commendation from James Pace, Commander of the USS

Banner.

The USS Banner was designated a target ship for the nuclear test series labeled Operation Crossroads. The detonation site was at Bikini Atoll, on July 25, 1946, and the ship suffered extensive damage. What remained of the USS Banner was scuttled in deep water off Kwajalein Atoll on February 16, 1948, and its name was erased from the Navy list of ships less than a month later.

The ship that carried him into the South Pacific battle zone had met its end, but for Glenn Morris, the end was still twenty-six years away.

The Descent from Olympus

The courage shown by soldiers during the island campaigns became legend, said U.S. Admiral Chester Nimitz of the U.S. Marines who fought at Iwo Jima. That statement also applies to all those who fought in the islands. There, Nimitz said in a report echoed by the National Archives, "common valor was a common virtue." *(32)*

Valor is most certainly a virtue, but during World War II it did not come without high cost. After being discharged from the service, Morris found himself in a world he could not adjust easily to. The gold and the glory were long gone, replaced with hostile memories of shattered dreams and a horrific war experience. He had seen men die all around him. Like the opening minutes of the film "Saving Private Ryan" showed with such excruciating power, survival in the heat of battle is merely a terrible game of chance. Who survives and who dies, who keeps his limbs intact and who doesn't, is left almost entirely to chance.

Most men who came back from World War II considered themselves real-life proof of the theme in a Bill Mauldin cartoon. Mauldin became famous for his "Willie and Joe" etchings depicting life for soldiers in the war. In one of the most famous cartoons, the two soldiers are seen crouching in battle gear as bullets whiz by overhead: "I feel like a fugitive from the law of averages," says one of the characters.

When a woman asked Audie Murphy, the most decorated soldier in World War II, what he was "commonly called" he responded, "a fugitive from the law of averages." *(33)*

For a man like Morris, who worked incredibly hard for all he had attained and who had once believed that determination and a solid work ethic made the difference in men's fates, it must have been a very painful realization. In war, what mattered most was luck....not what you were willing to do to try and achieve success. Drive, determination and persistence meant little; anyone who survived was merely lucky, a fugitive from the law of averages.

Returning to civilian life, Glenn decided to stay in California, giving up the Colorado part of his life forever. He drifted from job to job, mostly as a steelworker or construction laborer. He reportedly began to suffer from hallucinations as the war experience began to reappear in his daydreams and night dreams. The pain of life was working to overwhelm the wonderful joys he had known as a youth in Simla and as a young man in Fort Collins.

"That lives with you, it is part of your body and soul," said Senator Chuck Hyde of Nebraska, during a talk show in 2001, in a discussion of war's negative effect on soldiers. "It's the haunting effect that stays with you."

That Glenn was haunted by his war experiences seems beyond doubt. He was damaged psychologically, but he was also suffering physically, as well.

"He just wasn't in good health," said his sister, Virginia Baxter. "He came back from the war with a lung infection and a heart murmur. He told me stories....about standing on the bridge all through the night, keeping watch, breathing in the cool air. He endured a lot. Of course, there were other men that did the same. He found that out in the hospital."

She sighed, then added, "You do what you can to get through it."

An inordinate share of his time was spent in a veterans hospital as Glenn attempted to reconstruct a life devastated by war and a stunning collapse of what were once magnificent fortunes. The shock of World War II was too powerful for him to shake off; deep in his subconscious, he was suffering from all he had seen and endured.

"Glenn was strange; he got in the vets hospital and just couldn't pull himself away from it," Jack said. "We lived in Danville then, not far away from the hospital in Palo Alto where Glenn went most of the time. We had a swimming pool in our backyard and Glenn would come over some weekends. He loved to swim.

"But we had to be careful what members of the family we invited at the same time. We had to be very selective, because Glenn would flare up. There would be some very uncomfortable scenes. He would say some things that hurt, and then go into a room and seclude himself."

One explanation for such behavior may be found in the pages of *Achilles in Vietnam: Combat Trauma and the Undoing of Character*:

"A person 'broken' by combat has lost the capacity for a sense of well-being, self-respect, confidence and satisfaction — all attributes that we lump together in our concept of happiness," wrote Shay. *(34)* Shay offers numerous accounts of how difficult it is for veterans who have seen extensive action to readjust to civilian life.

"Audie, Elvis and (Howard) Hughes were all representatives of American dreams gone astray," wrote Don Graham in explaining how the gold and the glory can disappear so quickly. *(35)* He could have added Glenn Morris to that list, as well. Morris apparently could not make the transition from life that was so glorious in its quest and attainment, and life that was so empty and meaningless after the devastation of the dreams he had harbored prior to World War II.

His brothers, former Olympic teammates, and even Byron "Whizzer" White recall Glenn Morris in much the same manner — a man with a wealth of natural talent, given to brief periods of joviality; but mostly a man unsure of what the future held in store for him, and perhaps losing confidence in his ability to cope with life's swiftly shifting favors.

Ernie Pyle lived with the soldiers and sailors of World War II, and eventually died with them. David Nichols, in his biography of Pyle, entitled *Ernie's War*, explained that Pyle understood how war acts upon men in its own hideous way, and transforms them forever:

"Repeatedly he warned readers their sons and husbands were changed men, that what they endured was inconceivable to an outsider, and that patience and under-standing must be the hallmarks of their homecoming."

In the 1946 movie "The Best Years of Our Lives," all three of the main charac-ters are forced to deal with readjustment to the "civilized" world they had left behind to enter the war. In one scene, one of the characters has nightmares about a buddy who died during a plane attack. Starring Dana Andrews, Fredric March, Harold Russell and Myrna Loy, the movie touched a nerve in America and was a huge success. It won seven Academy Awards, including Best Picture of the Year.

The best line may have been one that Glenn Morris could certainly identify with: "Last year it was kill Japs, this year it's make money."

The 50th anniversary of D-Day was a worldwide television event in June of 1994, and the airwaves were filled with retrospectives of all sorts. One of the most poignant moments came when a soldier told about himself and his buddy hitting the beach, and the ensuing destruction and carnage. In faltering voice, he told of seeing his buddy hit, and then standing there, with his back to him. Finally, the buddy turned toward him, with one arm gone and half his face missing.

"Then, he turned and walked away, into the smoke," said the survivor, his voice trembling. "He just disappeared....and part of me disappeared with him."

No doubt, thousands of war survivors could relate to such a story. Perhaps a part of Glenn Morris disappeared on the beaches of the South Pacific as he saw many com-rades fall and die.

The other Olympic Tarzans – Weissmuller, Crabbe and Brix – all escaped the trauma of World War II as the government turned down all volunteers over the age of thirty. While Morris was twenty-nine at the time of his enlistment, Weissmuller was thirty-three when the Japanese bombed Pearl Harbor on Dec. 7, 1941, and Crabbe was thirty-two. Brix, the elder statesman of the group, was going on thirty-six. Their fighting was confined to the silver screen.

"World War II was a popular war – especially after it was clear the Allies were winning," reported *Newsweek*. "A kind of gaiety and excitement swept the country. Hollywood's dream factory shifted to a war footing with patriotic pap like 'Action in the North Atlantic' and 'The Purple Heart.'"

Ironically, the fictional Tarzan was given an opportunity to strike back at the offending nations. Burroughs' hero was such an international symbol for justice that the United States government requested that producer Sol Lesser manage somehow to get Tarzan involved in the war effort.

The state department "considered Tarzan an important propaganda weapon," wrote Gabe Essoe in his book, *Tarzan of the Movies*. "They were most eager to have films show that democracy will (triumph) only if it is alive and active, not compla-cently inert in its corner of the world." *(36)*

In Weissmuller's 1943 movie, "Tarzan Triumphs," the Nazis invaded the African jungle looking for raw materials they could use to aid their war effort. Tarzan's ini-tial reaction to the intrusion was a simple, "Nazi go away." But when the Nazis pushed him too far, the apeman responded in a fashion moviegoers had been anxiously antic-ipating: "Now Tarzan make war."

"At this point, audiences literally got to their feet and cheered. Tarzan's commando tactics brought the film to a thrilling finish," reported Essoe. It was a combined macho man/patriotic theme that Sylvester Stallone would resurrect in the 1980s with fabulous success as a character named Rambo.

"Tarzan's Triumph" was such a hit that Lesser followed less than a year later with "Tarzan's Desert Mystery," pitting the jungle lord against the evil Nazis once again; and with similar results. Weissmuller also made a cameo role as Tarzan in "Stage Door Canteen," a film which starred Ronald Reagan and was designed to drum up support for the war effort. Combining a future president and the jungle hero in the film was a nice touch; Reagan read many a Tarzan book while growing up in his hometown of Dixon, Illinois.

John Wayne and Audie Murphy emerged as the reel and real heroes of World War II, Wayne earning movie immortality with his larger-than-life characterizations on the screen, and Murphy doing the real thing on the battlefields of Europe before moving on to Hollywood himself for a film career. Other Hollywood stars were also involved in war films in the 1940s.

Brix, now known as Bruce Bennett, made ten films during the war years. He had starring roles in five war films, playing heroic naval officers twice. His wartime movie with the greatest impact came in 1943. It starred Humphrey Bogart, with Bennett in the second male lead. "Sahara" was a tale of an American tank squad fighting the Nazis in North Africa.

As a result of their Olympic performances, the four superb athletes earned varying amounts of gold and glory during the 1930s. They had moved smoothly from the wild acclaim that accompanies magnificent athletic achievement to the bright lights of Hollywood stardom. As Tarzans, they had become the idols of millions of young men and women around the world.

But none of their successes prepared them for the disappointments that lay in hiding during the 1940s. The passage of years brought on the unavoidable decline of their magnificent athletic prowess; hence, the diminishing of their tremendous physical appeal on the screen was a psychological jolt difficult to cope with. Though Bennett became a top character actor, the other three were unable to follow suit. As his expanding waistline and sagging muscles jeopardized his future, Weissmuller began to search for an identity. When the film world turned its back on the serials and "B" movies Crabbe had excelled in for over a decade, he found himself struggling to fit into the ever-changing Hollywood scene.

Morris was caught in the most debilitating circumstances of all. Since the magnificent triumphs of Berlin, he had gone from one traumatic disappointment to another. Neither film nor professional sports had offered the security or contentment he sought. World War II put him on a downhill roller coaster ride from which he couldn't escape. Like millions of others, he would never fully recover from the ravages of World War II. The unending loneliness of the Pacific and the combat experiences had combined with his own sensitive and introspective nature to extract a terrible toll.

"That which is most unendurable in war – the awful, ordinary, daily routine of war – is relegated to those dim regions where men hide all bad memories," wrote Jean

Larteguy, a French soldier and journalist. "But those memories survive, no matter how deeply buried, and sometimes they emerge." The demons lodged deep in Morris's memory were destined to emerge time after time in the years ahead.

Jack related a story that provides an insight to the turmoil swirling in Glenn's mind.

"My sister, Theda, wanted to help out more and to get him involved in society," said Jack. "She decided to pick him up one day, from the Palo Alto Hospital, and just take him for a ride.

"Not long into the ride, she noticed Glenn was staring out the rider's side of the window, and seemed real intent. Then he started shouting for her to pull over the car. They were in Chinatown, and he saw a group of Chinese. He thought they were Japanese. He started cursing, and yelling at them. He was in a real high state of anxiety, and she was very frightened. She stopped the car, and he jumped out and ran off. She never took him out again."

In the book *Achilles in Vietnam*, Shay wrote that such experiences are common among veterans suffering from post-traumatic stress syndrome. And the effects can be mind-numbing.

"…unhealed PTSD can devastate life and incapacitate its victims from participation in the domestic, economic and political life of the nation. The painful paradox is that fighting for one's country can render one unfit to be its citizen." *(37)*

"I come across veterans of World War II who still break down and cry when they are talking about memories of World War II," said Massachusetts Senator John Kerry, some 55 years after the war had ended.

But, not all veterans suffered from such agonies. One who apparently managed to adjust well was Maurice Britt, who returned to Arkansas as a highly-decorated soldier and built a very successful family life and career. Though he lost an arm in battle, he became the state's attorney general. In the book *No Name on the Bullet*, he is quoted about his feelings on war.

"A lot of young men had trouble adjusting," said Britt. "The mystery is why some did and some didn't." *(38)*

Author Don Graham paints a vivid portrait of Audie Murphy's grim struggle with the memories of war…. "of a psyche troubled by combat experiences." He drove cars way too fast, fired guns at objects in strange hours, prowled the streets of cities late at night, and suffered from nightmares. He told his sister once that he "didn't sleep a minute last night, I fought the damned war all night long." *(39)*

"War robs you mentally and physically," said Murphy. "It drains you." *(40)*

That Glenn Morris's life should have slid downhill so sharply suggests that he was most certainly a victim of that terrible robbery. It seems safe to say that he never recovered from the horrors he saw on beaches in the Pacific Rim. The young boy who grew up strong and sturdy on a small Colorado ranch was simply unprepared for what he encountered in World War II, just as Audie Murphy, a boy who grew up on a dirt ranch in Texas, was unprepared for what he saw and did.

On August 6, 1945, the Enola Gay flew over the industrial city of Hiroshima, at a height of 25,000 feet. Colonel Paul Tibbits was at the controls of the B-29 bomber, and released the atomic bomb that changed the world. Known as "Little Boy," the bomb produced what has been described as "a blinding fireball that incinerated everything within a three-mile radius, including 80,000 people." Just three days later, Nagasaki was leveled by another atomic bomb….and the Japanese offered to surrender the very next day.

Euphoria swept the world, and particularly the United States. The nation was in the mood to enjoy the fruits of its hard-earned victory. Thousands upon thousands of veterans returned, looking for work or to use the GI Bill and gain a college education. Television exploded onto the scene, bringing with it new entertainment stars – ranging from comedians like Sid Caesar and Milton Berle to professional wrestlers like Lou Thesz and Gorgeous George. Many veterans opted to take the 52-20 plan, drawing discharge benefits of $20 a week for an entire year.

Back in civilian life, Glenn was struggling to find himself once again. He wasn't in much demand as a former sports celebrity, but he was invited to appear at a ceremony in Tulare, California, in September of 1948. The event was to honor Tulare's Bob Mathias, who had stunned the world by winning the Olympic decathlon title in London, at the mere age of seventeen! Mathias had won the gold medal with a total point score of 7,189, considerably less than the 7,900 Morris had racked up twelve years earlier in Berlin. At the banquet, Morris drew a strong ovation when he said, "When my decathlon record is broken, I hope Bob will do it."

Many years later, Mathias still fondly remembered the meeting with Morris, and enjoyed the time he had spent with the world record holder. "I saw no signs of the problems that apparently hit him later on," said Mathias. "But then, I was just a young kid. I remember after he left, my dad saying what a nice guy he was, and I certainly agreed."

The meeting with Morris, and Glenn's tremendous records, played a key role in Mathias staying with the decathlon another four years.

"When I got back home, I realized that I didn't know a lot about the history of the Olympics, and especially any details about the decathlon itself, or the people who had competed in this event in Olympics past," said Mathias. "I did know the name of Glenn Morris, and that he set the Olympic and World record in the 1936 Games, but I hadn't seen his actual marks for each of the ten events when he set the record.

"After the London Games, I really thought that I would not compete in any more decathlons. Training was hard and time consuming and the 1952 Helsinki Games were four long years way. But when I finally saw Glenn's marks for the ten events, I changed my mind! His results so inspired me that from that moment Glenn became my idol and hero.

"I looked at his time in the 100 meters and thought that if I worked real hard for the next four years I could maybe run it as fast as he had. I did the same for the other nine events – and suddenly, for the first time in my life, I had a goal. That goal was to try to equal or better the marks of my newly-found idol. Somehow, two years later at a national decathlon meet in Tulare, I did break his world record. Then at the 1952 Helsinki Olympics, I broke his Olympic Games record, and also broke my own world record.

"I would not have continued with the decathlon if it hadn't been for the inspiration that Glenn provided in his great performance in 1936. I always give credit to my coach, and to Glenn Morris, for helping me with the decathlon."

Like many war veterans, Morris found it very difficult to adjust to civilian life. But he also seemed to be experiencing tremendous angst in accepting the fact that his glory years were long gone. In the 1950s, he worked some as a steel rigger for the Atomic Energy Commission at the Nevada testing grounds. He then found employment as a construction worker but was being bothered by nagging health problems. He began to float from job to job, with long intervals between work. His sister, Virginia Baxter, recalled that her once-famous brother worked off and on as a parking lot attendant at an airport, and as a security guard for several years.

During his last decade of life, Glenn was in and out of the Veterans Health Care System facility in Palo Alto, California. He was suffering from psychological distress, and from physical illnesses. Departing from the active physical life he had known for decades, he had stopped exercising completely and turned into a heavy smoker.

He married for a second time in the 1950s, but the marriage didn't last long. Even Virginia, who was probably closer to him than anyone else at the time, doesn't remember the woman's name for certain, or much about her.

"I only met her two or three times," said Virginia in 2001. "Her name might have been Lynn and I think she was a waitress, but I'm not sure. I think she was from the Sacramento area, but I don't really remember any more. I know it didn't last very long. They were living in the Long Beach area, but she wanted to go back to Sacramento to be with her children, and that's what she did."

Glenn's early retirement was brought on through disability and he was a member of the Disabled American Veterans. He spent lots of time alone, and lived at the Veterans Center Home at 795 Willow Road in Menlo Park, California, a town some thirty miles from San Francisco. He seldom traveled, but enjoyed spending time with Virginia, who lived about thirty miles away in San Mateo.

William Ball, media director at the Palo Alto Veterans Health Care System, said records from the pre-1975 era were destroyed in a fire.

"Menlo Park is considered a psychological facility, with definitely a psych component," said Ball in 2001. "If a person couldn't fit into society and was a veteran, that's where they went. The VA took care of them. It was some way for them to try and lead a normal life.

"We call such a problem 'post-traumatic stress disorder' now," he said. "Back then (in the World War II era), it was called 'shell shock.' Some of the patients would have assignments, in an incentive therapy program. They probably did that in exchange for a stipend of some sorts." *(41)*

After moving into the Vets Hospital, Glenn worked in the laundry unit during the ten years or so he lived at the facility. In the final years of his life, Morris certainly had ample opportunity to reflect back on what was….and what might have been.

"I think his faith in God got him through," said Virginia. "He had a great faith in the Almighty, and thought anything was possible through God. I think that's what carried him through the rough times. I asked him once, 'Glenn, do you ever pray?' And he said, 'Yes, I do. Why, I pray all the time.' We both liked to attend the Stanford chapel, and we would go together."

Their faith was a continuation of the education they had received from their father and mother back in Simla. "John and Emma weren't Bible thumpers, so to speak, but they shared their strong faith and belief in God with their children," wrote Jean Bird. "They read scriptures from the Bible and explained them to their children." *(42)*

His final years of life were spent enjoying the simple things. Again, as a youth, it was his love of sport that helped see him through.

"He kept up with everyday sports, and liked to watch football games on TV," said Virginia. "He was a fan of the San Francisco 49ers, the Dallas Cowboys and, of course, the team he played for, the Detroit Lions. And the Olympics, he always watched the Olympics when they came around."

She remembers that he had a subtle sense of humor – "but you had to be on your toes to stay with him" – and was a steady reader. He was particularly interested in anything that had to do with unidentified flying objects (UFOs).

"I used to think, 'What is he interested in that for?'" she recalled with a slight chuckle. "But he really was. He would read anything he could get his hands on about UFOs, and was always interested in investigating the subject.

"He was an intelligent man who liked to think about things. He just went along peacefully through life."

There were fleeting moments when he would be reminded of his great accomplishments. One such time came in 1969 when he received word he was being inducted into the Colorado Sports Hall of Fame. Betty Kaatz, a sister living in Hayward, Calif., wrote to a Simla newsman expressing how her brother felt: "He has received so many notes and cards and is very honored with the recognition bestowed on him." But, she added, "he has a back problem and emphysema acutely which prevents his making a trip to Denver for the banquet."

The man once considered the world's greatest athlete was a mere shell of himself by the time the 1970s arrived. Though longevity was common in the Morris family (both of his parents and all of his siblings reached age 80, at least), by age sixty he was seriously ill. He was suffering from an enlarged heart, emphysema and high blood pressure. According to Jean Bird, "he developed a severe case of bronchitis, which brought about complications and resulted in heart failure." *(43)*

Jack and his wife, Althea, visited Glenn regularly in his final weeks. On January 31, 1974, they were at the hospital in the morning; then, acting on a hunch, they decided to return again in the evening. Jack let Althea out at the main entrance and drove away to park the car. Althea entered Glenn's room alone, and he smiled weakly when he saw her. He was in the closing moments of his life.

By the time Jack made it to the room, Glenn had died. Althea was there alone. She said that the very last words Glenn spoke to her were: "Who would have ever thought I'd go out like this?"

Jack sighed as he recalled the moment, and then continued: "He once told me, 'You know, I should have stayed with Leni in Germany. That was the biggest mistake of my life.'"

The heart that had pumped so furiously and efficiently through years of hard work and athletic success had finally worn out. Funeral services for Glenn Morris were held in St. Andrews Church in Burlingame, with arrangements by the Crosby and Gray Mortuary of Burlingame. He was buried in Skylawn Memorial Park.

Today, his great athletic accomplishments, in perhaps the most intriguing of all Olympic Games, have been largely forgotten. By the year 2002, hardly anyone other than the most dedicated athletic scholar knows anything about the Colorado comet.

"He felt like all he had done was pretty much forgotten," said Virginia. "He wondered if anyone cared, if it all really mattered. We went shopping in a mall once, and he stopped suddenly and looked around. He said, 'Once I was the world's greatest athlete, and no one here knows or cares.'"

"Part of the problem is the decathlon just didn't get the attention back then that it does now," said Marty Glickman, a 1936 Olympian who went on to a long and successful career in broadcasting. "Glenn did not get the play that the other winners did. He was an also-ran in that respect."

Glenn Morris had a lot in common with his first sports idol, the great Jim Thorpe. Not only were they both superb all-around athletes and gold medal decathletes, but their post-Olympic personal lives and disappointments were similar.

"Unfortunately, the glory, fame and recognition of his athletic accomplishments did not bring him happiness," wrote Grace Thorpe of her father. "His personal life was sad..." *(44)*

The life of Glenn Morris took a sad turn, as well. Leni Riefenstahl and Hollywood certainly played a role, but World War II was probably the primary cause of the downturn. Around the world, an estimated fifty million people died because of the war....and millions more suffered physical or psychological pain the rest of their lives. Morris was fortunate that he escaped physical injury, but the psychological damage was devastating. Once Morris became engulfed in the total madness and ferocity of war and saw its devastation up close and personal, he could not recover. But his life was set on a downward course even earlier, according to several who knew him best. It appears the decision to cast his fortune in Hollywood was a significant factor as well.

"He never thought he was treated fairly and he was angry at his agent," said Virginia.

"I think he was disenchanted by the Hollywood experience," said Norman Cable, his former football pupil. "Anyone would have been. It looked like big things were going to happen, and then it all disappeared." *(45)*

"His life in Hollywood wasn't anything," said Ken Carpenter, Olympic discus champion in 1936. "They exploited him to the utmost." *(46)*

Carpenter, who said he was being considered for the Tarzan role himself at one point, apparently believed that the combination of the disappointment in Hollywood and the trauma of World War II had a debilitating effect on Morris's life. Harry Hughes, Glenn's coach and close confidant at Colorado State College, was among the many friends who were baffled by Glenn's declining fortunes.

"Harry talked so much of Glenn, what a wonderful athlete he was," wrote Hughes' widow, Ruby, in 1979. "He really loved that boy and grieved over him. I don't think he knew what really happened to him in his later years. So sad." *(47)*

Richard Beidleman came through his experiences as an officer on the USS Banner in much better fashion than Morris. Beidleman adjusted easily to civilian life, and began a career as an educator. He taught biology at Colorado State University in the 1950s, where Morris had excelled two decades earlier. He wound up his career at Colorado College in Colorado Springs, retiring in 1988 and moving to California.

"I often wondered what happened to Glenn Morris," said Beidleman in 2001. "I didn't hear much about him after the war. He was a complex personality, that's for sure. Maybe part of the explanation is his upbringing on the farm. I had lots of young kids from the farms in my classes, and they had attitudes like, 'If the pigs can understand me, that's all that matters.'

Trying to rise above their poverty-level early life is a common theme in the stories of many great athletic figures of the Morris era. The 2002 HBO movie, "The Junction City Boys," discusses some elements of the career of football coaching legend Paul "Bear" Bryant. He apparently also grappled with the poverty issue all of his adult life.

"It (his poor upbringing) ate at him, gnawed at him, his whole life," said author Mickey Herskowitz on a talk show after the movie. "Winning meant so much to Bear Bryant because his life had been so hard."

Another author, John Underwood, agreed: "Coach Bryant has his way, which was a reflection of his upbringing."

The same can be said of Glenn Morris.

"In retrospect, I can sympathize with Glenn better now than I did when we were on the Banner," said Beidleman. "He came from a small farm and suddenly was hot stuff, up there on the world stage....being an Olympic champion and Tarzan. But when I met him, he was having problems trying to adjust to the fact that his star had set. He was a very important figure in the 1930s, but by the 1940s, and after that, he wasn't so important anymore. That must have been very difficult for him to accept."

Virginia feels that Glenn's life would have turned out far differently had he stayed with NBC radio back in 1937.

"He loved sports and would have been good at that," she said. "Unfortunately, he made a bad decision. He left NBC and went to Hollywood, and he really didn't have any guidance, or an older person to turn to for advice. He was alone in a tough world. His agent gave him some bad advice, and it wasn't his kind of world out there.

"He had a lot in his hand....and it went through his hand like sand."

TOP: Lieutenant Glenn Morris stands in the front row at the far right in this photo of officers and men of the U.S.S. Banner. The photo is from Dr. Richard G. Beidleman, standing to the right of Morris.

BELOW: The U.S.S. Banner, circa 1942.

LEFT: Lt. Glenn Morris stands behind two of the sailors in his crew on the U.S.S. Banner

BELOW: The same photo, with Lt. Morris at the far left.

(Photos courtesy of Richard Beidleman)

Jim Larson (left) and Reed Lake
served on the USS Banner with
Morris. Larson participated in a
wild scene with Lt. Morris during
the landing at White Beach.

Ready for battle, Morris signed this
photo of himself to a man who
served under him.

These are the types of guns that were firing all day and all night when
Lt. Morris was on duty during fighting in Lingayen Gulf.

In this photo, American troops pour out of the landing craft
style of ships that Glenn Morris served on during World War
II. These troops are landing on Red Beach at Morotai Island
in the Philippines on September of 1944. The USS Banner
bypassed this beach but saw terrible action on White Beach
in December of 1944.

(Photo from U.S. Navy photo book)

TOP: This is the type of landing scene that Morris and his men from the USS Banner would have been involved with throughout the South Pacific.

LEFT: Marines inch forward against suicidal resistance on an island in the South Pacific.

(Photos from U.S. Navy photo book)

TOP: The South College Gym where Glenn trained for the 1936 Olympics is now used as a physical education facility on the Colorado State University campus. The CSU track teams also are headquartered here.

The high school in Simla has several trophy cases devoted to telling the story of its most famous graduate. Glenn's gold medal is also at the school.

Glenn Morris (right) visited with Bob Mathias (center) and his father (left) in the Mathias home in Tulare, California. Bob was being honored by his hometown for winning the Olympic decathlon title in London in 1948. Glenn was a special guest for the event.

(Photo courtesy of Bob Mathias)

This photo was taken in 1974, when Glenn was 62 years old and near the end of his life. Glenn died on January 31, 1974, in Palo Alto, California, from heart failure. He had been suffering from several ailments for many years.

Postscript

Like his days on earth, the memories of Glenn Morris seem to rise and fall like a roller coaster ride. Largely forgotten by all but the most devout Olympic and Tarzan fans, he surfaces from time to time, only to disappear quickly from view.

In December of 1988, *The Olympian* magazine printed an article about Morris aptly labeled "The Forgotten Olympian." Eleven years later, a sportswriter for the Fort Collins Coloradoan newspaper, offering an "athlete of the century" list for his readers, picked the top ten athletes in Fort Collins and Colorado State University history. Glenn Morris was No. 1 on the list, ahead of several former NFL stars, including one who is a member of the NFL hall of fame.

In 1999, *Sports Illustrated* produced a special issue in which it ranked the top fifty athletes in all fifty states. Morris was listed fourth in the state of Colorado – behind Jack Dempsey, Byron "Whizzer" White and Amy Van Dyken, an Olympic swimming champion.

"People might not remember him anymore, but Glenn Morris is still the greatest athlete this state has ever had,"" said Frank Haraway, a retired sportswriter for the Denver Post, in 1996.

One of the best accounts of his life came on June 30, 2002, in a Denver Post story written by Mike Burrows. In the story, Burrows quotes Cledys Moore of Simla: "War can change a man and I know it changed Glenn. From what I was told, he was never the same."

Burrows also quoted Bob Mathias, who expressed once again his great admiration for Glenn.

"The two names I heard about growing up were Jim Thorpe and Glenn Morris," said Mathias. He added that he went after Glenn's record in the decathlon after winning the gold medal himself in 1948. "They were super numbers, especially when you consider how few decathlons he competed in."

Yet, there is today scant reference to him on the Colorado State University campus. The field where he ran track meets and where he spent countless hours preparing or the Berlin Olympics is still in use. Athletes walk down the narrow hallway he traversed and step into a small, circular indoor track arena to work out. But there is no mention on the walls of Glenn Morris, to let the hopefuls of today know they are walking in the footsteps of an athlete who shook the foundations of the sports world in 1936.

A small track meet hosted by Colorado State University each spring is named in his honor. In 1999, there was a move under way to rename the small arena on South

College the Glenn Morris Fieldhouse. Dr. Bob Pike, a long-time Colorado State and Fort Collins booster, was leading the movement and was determined to see that the honor was bestowed on Glenn. But Dr. Pike died suddenly in the summer of 2000, and the project withered away.

Prior to the 1996 Olympics, the United States Olympic Committee issued a variety of tee shirts. One of them boasted the image of Glenn Morris throwing the javelin. Morris's athletic flame burned hot, but briefly, especially in the decathlon. He set either a world or Olympic mark in his only three attempts, and his 7,900 mark in Berlin stood fourteen years, before finally broken by Mathias in 1950. By retiring after Berlin's fabulous showing, he has left sports historians to ponder what might have been.

"One can only wonder what Morris would have done to the record book had he maintained an interest in the decathlon," wrote Frank Zarnowski. *(48)*

Morris Ververs has worked hard to keep the name of Glenn Morris alive in Simla and the surrounding area. Distantly related to Glenn through his wife, Verna, Ververs served as principal at Simla Union High School from 1967 through 1975. Determined that students should know at least something about the inspirational life of Glenn Morris, Ververs made contact with Jack Morris, and then drove out to San Diego to meet Jack and Althea.

"Jack gave us Glenn's gold medal, and lots of other memorabilia, including high school ribbons and medals," said Ververs. "We wanted them to be on display at the high school, and so did Jack and Althea."

The school began the Glenn Morris Athlete of the Year Award in 1975, which is given annually to the top athlete in the school. It was Ververs' goal to keep alive the memory of the town's most famous citizen and to inspire Simla's youth to dare to dream and strive to be the best. Bob Mathias was the featured speaker at the banquet where the Glenn Morris Award was introduced for the first time.

Today, Glenn Morris's Olympic gold medal from Berlin rests in the vault at the principal's office at Simla High School. Various other medals, ribbons and an assortment of photos are on display in the trophy case near the main gymnasium. On the outskirts of town, a sign on a softball field boasts that Simla is the hometown of NFL football star Barry Hilton (who won two Super Bowl rings as a punter with the San Francisco 49ers), of several state championship high school teams, and of 1936 Olympic champion Glenn Morris.

The boarding house where he lived in Fort Collins while training for the decathlon has been torn down, and the Village Shoe Repair shop sits in its place. The owner of the business, Joe Perry, is a pleasant man who had never heard of Glenn Morris prior to being asked questions about him in the fall of 2001.

"No kidding....an Olympic champion lived right here?" said Perry, when told of Morris's accomplishments. "And he even played Tarzan in the movies? Well, that's really something. I think we should put up a photo of him, so that people who come in will learn about him."

But Morris does have a presence on E-bay, the national selling phenomenon. Videos of "Tarzan's Revenge" are listed almost daily and on February 9, 2001, a

Glenn Morris autograph attracted twenty-five bids and sold for $192.

From 1936 through 1938 there was so much gold and glory for Glenn Morris that it seemed neither would ever fade. It took the world's greatest calamity, World War II, to bring him down from Olympus.

"Some people may have thought he was arrogant because he was so quiet, but he was a shy, introspective person," said Virginia. "I think he was put here on earth for a special reason. Glenn's greatest contribution was to help win that war. A lot of people made deep sacrifices, and Glenn was in the front row."

Part of his legacy is addressed in Tom Brokaw's magnificent best seller, *The Greatest Generation*.

"When I first came to fully understand what effect members of the World War II generation had on my life and the world we occupy today, I quickly resolved to tell their stories as a small gesture of personal appreciation," Brokaw wrote at the outset. *(49)* What followed was a powerful testimony to the young men and women who sacrificed everything they had, and were, in the noblest quest of all – freedom.

Tom Hanks, the star of "Saving Private Ryan" and one of the finest actors in movie history, understands the full commitment young Americans made by fighting in World War II. He has lent his name to an effort to have a World War II memorial built on the Washington Memorial mall.

"Incredibly, there is still no national memorial to honor the achievements of this great generation," he said in a national advertisement. "It's time to say thank you."

The life of Glenn Morris is a part of that generation, a part of that story….a part of that sacrifice. He rose from humble origins and, through pure hard work and determination, became the world's greatest athlete, a movie Tarzan, a NFL football player and a World War II hero. Five decades later, it may well be the stirring athletic achievements which best serve to measure the quality and impact of his life.

Sparks Alfred was a man who knew Morris well. As the business manager of the athletic department at Colorado State College, Alfred was on campus when Morris arrived in the fall of 1930. He saw him mature from a green college hopeful into the finest all-around athlete in the world.

"What made Glenn Morris?" Alfred asked rhetorically, when visited by Morris Ververs near the end of Sparks's life, and long after Morris had died.

"Glenn Morris made Glenn Morris! He outworked everyone, he drove himself to succeed. Many a night when the rest of the boys were out partying or doing whatever, Glenn was at the gym, working on the high jump, or running laps, or doing something. He had this incredible drive in him to be the best. He drove himself."

"I believe you can do almost anything you are willing to work hard enough for," Morris said near the end of his life. "In a year and a half prior to the Olympics, I didn't miss a dozen days working out. I let practically nothing interfere with my daily practices."

At the time of his death, eulogies were served up around Colorado, and the nation. "His saga as the world's greatest athlete served as an inspiration to countless Colorado youngsters of a later generation," wrote a Denver sportswriter.

Ironically, a beautiful book published in 1994 by St. Martin's Press, features a large facial photo of Morris on the back cover....with the name of the book OLYMPIA: LENI RIEFENSTAHL running across his features!

Today all that remains are ghostly memories and brief notations in a few books that record the deeds of the special few Americans who will forever be known as Olympic champions. And there the name of Glenn Morris will endure for as long as mankind follows sport. Bob Mathias himself summed it up this way:

"Everything about Glenn Morris seems incredible!"

Glenn Morris Highlights:

June 18, 1912 — Born the second of seven children to John and Emma Morris.

May 30, 1930 — Graduates from Simla Union High School.

June 6, 1935 — Graduates from Colorado State College in Fort Collins.

April 17-18, 1936 — Wins decathlon title at Kansas Relays and sets American record.

June 26-27, 1936 — Wins decathlon Olympic trials in Milwaukee and sets world record.

August 7-8, 1936 — Wins Olympic decathlon gold medal in Berlin and sets world record with 7,900 points.

September 9, 1936 — Glenn Morris Day proclaimed in Colorado.

November 10, 1936 — Wins Sullivan Award as nation's top amateur athlete.

January 7, 1938 — "Tarzan's Revenge" premieres.

September 15, 1940 — Plays first and only game with Detroit Lions of NFL.

March 6, 1942 — Enters into United States Navy.

July 1, 1947 — Discharged from United States Navy.

February 27, 1969 — Inducted into Colorado Sports Hall of Fame.

January 31, 1974 — Dies in Palo Alto, California, at age of 62.

Fall, 1988 — Inducted into Colorado State University Hall of Fame.

January 21, 1998 — Inducted into Colorado High School Activities Hall of Fame.

Decorations for service during World War II:

Asiatic-Pacific Campaign Medal.

Bronze Service Star (two).

American Theater Campaign Medal.

World War II Victory Medal.

Philippine Liberation Ribbon with Bronze Service Star.

Letter of Commendation from Commander, USS Banner.

The U.S. team of Bob Clark (left), Glenn Morris (center) and Jack Parker won all three medals in the decathlon.

1936 Olympic Decathlon Results:

The Americans – Glenn Morris, Bob Clark and Jack Morris – won all the three medals in the decathlon at the 1936 Olympic Games in Berlin. Their scores in the individual events, and the points scored for each event, are as follows:

	Glenn Morris	Bob Clark	Jack Parker
100-meter dash	11.1 seconds	10.9 seconds	11.4 seconds
Broad jump	22'-10"& 13/32	25'-0"	23'-5/16"
400-meter run	49.4 seconds	50 seconds	53.3 seconds
Shot put	46'-2" & 33/64	41'-7" & 7/32	44'-4& 19/64"
High Jump	6'- 27/32"	5'-10" & 7/8	5'-10" & 7/8
110-meter hurdles	14.9 seconds	15.7 seconds	15.0 seconds
Discus throw	141'-4 & 7/64"	129'-2 & 53/64"	128'- & 54/64"
Pole Vault	11'-5 & 13/16"	12'-1 & 11/16"	11'-5 & 13/16"
Javelin throw	178'-10 & 1/2"	167'-4 &11/16"	185'-2 & 7/8"
1,500-meter run	4 min., 32.2 sec	4 min., 44.4 sec.	5 min., 7.8 sec.
TOTAL SCORE	7,900 points	7,601 points	7,275 points

The effort by Glenn Morris broke by 20 points his own world record set at the Olympic Trials in Milwaukee, Wisconsin, on June 27; it also broke the 1932 Olympic record set by Jim Bausch in Los Angeles. Glenn's record stood for 14 years, until it was finally broken at the 1950 national meet by Bob Mathias with a score of 8,042.

Footnotes:

1. *Traces of our Heritage: Copeland, Matlock, Morris*, by Jean S. Bird, 1980, page 317
2. ibid, page 318
3. ibid, page 318
4. ibid, page 318
5. American Olympic Committee Report, 1936, USOC, page 22
6. *The Olympic Story: Pursuit of Excellence*, by the Associated Press, Grolier Enterprises, 1979, page 142
7. *An Approved History of the Olympic Games*, by Bill Henry, G.P. Putnam's Sons, 1948, page 232
8. Telephone interview with author
9. *The Olympic Story: Pursuit of Excellence*, by the Associated Press, Grolier Enterprises, 1979, page 150
10. *The Nazi Olympics*, by Dr. Richard Mandell, Macmillan, 1991, page 138
11. ibid, page 171
12. *The Decathlon*, by Frank Zarnowski, Leisure Press, 1989, page 61
13. Jewish Student Online Research Center
14. *A Memoir, by Leni Riefenstahl*, St. Martin's Press, 1994, page 196
15. ibid, page 196
16. ibid, page 197
17. American Olympic Committee Report, 1936, USOC, page 84
18. *A Memoir, by Leni Riefenstahl*, St. Martin's Press, 1994, page 199
19. ibid, page 199
20. taped interview, courtesy of Lewis Carlson and John J. Fogarty, authors of *Tales of Gold*, Contemporary Books, Inc.
21. Phone interview with author, December 2000.
22. Phone interview with author, February, 2001
23. *Letter to author, October 15, 2002.*
24. *Olympics and Olympiads: A Chronology*, page 187
25. *Kings of the Jungle*, by David Fury, McFarland and Company, Inc., 1992, page 136
26. *Tarzan of the Movies*, by Gabe Essoe, The Citadel Press, 1968, page 104
27. *The Nazi Olympics*, by Dr. Richard Mandell, Macmillan, 1991, page 291
28. National Archives poster
29. ibid
30. *No Name on the Bullet*, by Don Graham, Penguin Books, 1989, page 126
31. *Colorado and its People*, page 590
32. National Archives
33. *No Name on the Bullet*, by Don Graham, Penguin Books, 1989, page 112

34. *Achilles in Vietnam: Combat Trauma and the undoing of Character*, Jonathan Shay, A Touchstone Book, 1994, page 174

35. *No Name on the Bullet*, by Don Graham, Penguin Books, 1989, page 345

36. *Tarzan of the Movies*, by Gabe Essoe, The Citadel Press, 1968, page 115

37. *Achilles in Vietnam: Combat Trauma and the undoing of Character*, Jonathan Shay, A Touchstone Book, 1994, page 83

38. *No Name on the Bullet*, by Don Graham, Penguin Books, 1989, page 119

39. ibid, page 123

40. ibid, page 124

41. telephone interview January 26, 2001

42. *Traces of Our Heritage: Copeland, Matlock, Morris*, by Jean S. Bird, page 31

43. ibid, page 329

44. *Jim Thorpe, World's Greatest Athlete*, Children's Press, 1984, page 7

45. Telephone interview, January 30, 2001

46. Taped interview, courtesy of Lewis Carlson and John J. Fogarty, authors of *Tales of Gold,* Contemporary Books, Inc.

47. Letter to Morris Ververs, November 15, 1979.

48. *The Decathlon*, by Frank Zarnowski, Leisure Press, 1989, page 72

49. *The Greatest Generation*, by Tom Brokaw, Random House, 1998.

Bibliography:

No Name on the Bullet, by Don Graham, Penguin Books, 1989.

The Greatest Generation, by Tom Brokaw, Random House, 1998.

Tarzan of the Movies, by Gabe Essoe, The Citadel Press, 1968.

Kings of the Jungle, by David Fury, McFarland and Company, Inc., 1992.

The Nazi Olympics, by Dr. Richard Mandell, Macmillan, 1991.

The Games of '36, by Stan Cohen, Pictorial Histories Publishing Company, 1996.

American Olympic Committee Report, 1936, USOC.

An Approved History of the Olympic Games, by Bill Henry, G.P. Putnam's Sons, 1948.

The Decathlon, by Frank Zarnowski, Leisure Press, 1989.

A Memoir, by Leni Riefenstahl, St. Martin's Press, 1994.

The Olympic Story: Pursuit of Excellence, by the Associated Press, Grolier Enterprises, 1979.

Jim Thorpe: World's Greatest Athlete, by Gregory Richards, Children's Press, 1984.

Bob Mathias: The Life of the Olympic Champion, by Myron Tassin, St. Martin's Press, 1983.

Traces of Our Heritage: Copeland, Matlock, Morris, by Jean S. Bird, 1980.

Achilles in Vietnam: Combat Trauma and the Undoing of Character, by Jonathon Shay, M.D., Ph.D., Touchstone Books, 1995

Interviews:

John (Jack) Morris, by phone, several times, 1988.
Wayne Morris, by phone, several times, 1988.
Morris Ververs, by phone, several times, 2000, 2001, 2002.
Frank Zarnowski, by phone December 5, 2000.
Dr. Richard Mandell, by phone, December, 2000.
Vernon Morris, by phone, December 10, 2000.
Morris Ververs, in Simla on January 16, 2001.
Cledys Moore in Simla on January 16, 2001.
J.J. (Swede) Moreland in Simla on January 16, 2001.
Virginia Morris Baxter, by phone, January 21, 2001.
Virginia Morris Baxter, by phone, February 10, 2001.
Caroline Edwards Tucker, by phone, January 21, 2001.
Bill Ball, by phone, January 26, 2001.
Norman V. Cable, by phone, January 30, 2001.
Eleanor Holm, by phone, February 9, 2001.
Jim Larson, by phone, December 16, 2001.
Jim Larson, at his Denver home, December 24, 2001.
Bob Mathias, in person, June 30, 2002.
Danton Burroughs, in person, September 1, 2002.
Harold "Rusty" Wilson Jr., by phone, September 17, 2002.

Letters

From Ruby Thompson to Morris Ververs, dated November 15, 1979.
From Supreme Court Justice Byron White, dated May 27, 1988.
From Bob Mathias, dated June 22, 1988.
From Wayne Morris, dated January 9, 1989.
From John (Jack) Morris, dated March 17, 1989.
From Jack Morris, dated February 26, 1991.
From Norman V. Cable, dated January 17, 2001.
From Leni Riefenstahl, dated October 15, 2002.

Index

How to order from
Culture House Books
To order this book or others published by Culture House Books, either call 614-526-8836, or email your questions to museum@pcpartner.net.

About the Author

In 2002, Mike Chapman retired from a 35-year career in newspapers, having served as a sports editor, managing editor, executive editor and publisher. His work has appeared in dozens of national and regional publications and he is a recognized authority on Tarzan and the sport of wrestling.

Currently the executive director of the International Wrestling Institute and Museum in Newton, Iowa, Mike and his wife Bev live in Kellogg, Iowa. They have three grown children.

The Gold and the Glory is his fourteenth book. His most recent book previously was *Please Don't Call Me Tarzan*, which is a biography of former Tarzan actor Herman Brix (aka Bruce Bennett).